Not So Golden State

Char Miller

Not So Golden State

Sustainability vs. the California Dream

Trinity University Press | SAN ANTONIO

Published by Trinity University Press
San Antonio, Texas 78212

Cover design by Sarah Cooper
Book design by DigiTek Publishing, Chennai, India

ISBN-13 978-1-59534-782-4 paper
ISBN-13 978-1-59534-783-1 ebook

Trinity University Press strives to produce its books using methods
and materials in an environmentally sensitive manner. We favor
working with manufacturers that practice sustainable management
of all natural resources, produce paper using recycled stock,
and manage forests with the best possible practices for people,
biodiversity, and sustainability. The press is a member of the Green
Press Initiative, a nonprofit program dedicated to supporting
publishers in their efforts to reduce their impacts on endangered
forests, climate change, and forest-dependent communities.

The paper used in this publication meets the minimum
requirements of the American National Standard for Information
Sciences—Permanence of Paper for Printed Library Materials,
ANSI 39.48-1992.

CIP data on file at the Library of Congress

20 19 18 17 16 | 5 4 3 2 1

Contents

Introduction

We tell stories. We tell stories about the land, about its contours and topographies. We read our way into it; we wonder about our place within its embrace, whether this place is as wide as the West or as narrow as a creek bed or sidewalk. Our imaginings of these spaces are at the base of how we interpret what we believe to be their meaning. There is nothing earth-shattering about this claim for the divining power of the human imagination, not least because the clues seem so omnipresent, just waiting to be seen, read, and told.

Like those visible each day to tens of thousands of Los Angeles commuters who creep along the Golden State Freeway (Interstate 5) as it swings through the Glendale Narrows, heading into downtown or San Fernando Valley. This pinch point in the city's sprawling urban geography frames the windshield—hills to the east and west create a pass that the Los Angeles River has carved over the millennia, a curving energy that, as David Brodsly observed in *LA Freeway: An Appreciative Essay*, established the "structural continuity" of transportation through this section of Los Angeles. Native peoples traveled along the river's broad banks to make use of the fifty-two-mile-long riparian corridor; at the confluence of the river and the Arroyo Seco, which helped shape the narrows, they established a settlement that later Spanish missionaries would appropriate into their community-development scheme. Horses, carriages, and wagons rolled along these same banks as a north–south passage that in time would be paved over with the construction of Riverside Drive just to the river's west; the eastern flatland was absorbed into the regional railroad grid, the site of the now-abandoned Taylor Yard. Arcing over this animated network is the Golden State, a fourth generation of movement scored into what Brodsly calls this "earthen tablet." When my students and I slop in the LA River beneath this revelatory junction point, we talk about being alert to such palimpsests that can reveal our dynamic engagement with the past.

There are other signals waiting to be interrogated, such as those I flashed past one fine spring day as I drove north on Interstate 5 up and over the Tehachapi Mountains and into the fertile Central Valley. Two sets of them lining the four-lane highway narrated competing stories about the drought wracking California in the second decade of the twenty-first century. The most in-your-face were the ubiquitous billboards and placards decrying the lack of water flowing to Big Ag operations that dominate the valley's economic activity. The culprit for this low(er) flow is not climate-driven drought but the U.S. Congress.

Some of the messages demonize particular politicians (Representative Nancy Pelosi remains a favorite target, though she has not been House Speaker for years). Most strike an ominous tone, as if a conspiracy is afoot: Stop the Congress Created Dust Bowl! No Water = No Jobs! No Water = Higher Food Prices! A handful of others encourage Southern Californians to see their shared pain; water restrictions bite just as hard in Kern and King Counties as they do in Los Angeles and San Diego.

Yet what was happening on the ground—the physical reality—offered a counternarrative to these signposts of a polarized and polarizing political landscape. Everywhere, water was on the move. Ditches fanning out from the State Water Project and the Central Valley Project were flush, a rush of white gold on its way to irrigate row crops, orchards, and groves. The sun glinted off flooded rice fields. Sprinklers arced across new beds that stretched out to the horizon, aerosoling the sky with a rainbow hue. Tractor and pickup tires were mud-encased.

The source of this water, amid a deepening drought, was puzzling. Since 2010, there have been well-announced cutbacks of water deliveries to urban and rural consumers dependent on the steadily shrinking Sierra snowpack. Industrial, residential, and agricultural users have been hyperalert to the impact of this five-year dry spell and in some cases have been actively involved in conservation initiatives, making do with less.

Not everyone has been so savvy or proactive. But it was not until I spotted an article in the *Modesto Bee* that I understood how some of the same folks shedding crocodile tears about reduced water deliveries are implicated in the problem they so vehemently denounce. "Irrigation districts provide water that's key to agricultural prosperity in the Northern San Joaquin Valley," noted reporter J. N. Sbranti in his front page, top-of-the-fold piece, "but some of those districts also have been cashing in on the region's water resources."

The amount of money involved is staggering. After digging into the relevant data, Sbranti calculated that local irrigation districts in San Joaquin, Stanislaus, and Merced Counties mined 1.5 million acre-feet of groundwater between 2004 and 2014 and then sold a significant portion to out-of-district agencies to the tune of $140 million. *Ka-ching!*

Surely that delightful sound is music to the ears of the managers of the Oakdale Irrigation District (OID), for example, in eastern Stanislaus County. Since 2004 it has sold 40,000 acre-feet for a tidy $35 million, a strategy that contained an odd wrinkle: "Despite having surplus water to sell from its Sierra reservoirs, OID continued to pump its Valley wells."

Why would it sell off hard-to-replenish groundwater instead of already available snowmelt? Why would it fill its coffers while seriously depleting local supplies? Why choose the short-term, if lucrative, fix when doing so will only exacerbate its long-term problem?

This district's actions, and those of its peers, are hard to fathom. Then again, maybe not. Diametrically opposed to any form of groundwater monitoring—which the state finally began to require in 2015—they have been making bank during the drought. The Westlands Water District, which is cash rich but water poor, has been an eager buyer of their waters, and in 2013 alone, it paid $4 million to OID for 40,000 acre-feet. At the same time it scooped up surplus supplies from Merced, Patterson, and West Stanislaus Districts, a spending spree that helped to drive this sharp increase in pumping.

What appeared to be an economic boon to the affected water districts quickly began to exact a steep cost. As Fresno State's Sarge Green told the *Modesto Bee*, when local aquifers are overdrafted, they start subsiding, a process that has long complicated life in the valley and will continue to do so as long as overpumping continues. With subsidence, water quality and quantity are also compromised.

Green also noted this irony: The Central Valley Project, whose concrete-lined canals now move around this newly pumped groundwater, was a New Deal–funded initiative designed in part to wean local farmers off that very finite supply. What those in the 1930s recognized, we have forgotten: once these aquifers are depleted, they cannot be reclaimed.

The social consequences of this environmental collapse will be profound, wreaking havoc on the Central

Valley's agricultural economy and disrupting its urban development, a drying up of options and a diminishing of opportunities—much as an earlier generation of farmers experienced after they laid down levees and pumped the once-massive Tulare Lake into but a memory. When that happens, when Big Ag and its irrigation-district allies start sucking up mud rather than water, what then?

That question, deliberately left hanging, is central to the narrative trope that runs through *Not So Golden State*. It probes the choices we have made and will make about how we wish to live, work, and recreate in this place we call the American West. About the choices that have led us to inhabit spaces urban, rural, and wild. Or to hunker down in the desert, press out to the beach, nestle into tight canyons, build atop foothills and ridgelines, and sprawl along valley floors. By making these disparate landscapes our home we complicate the natural systems that drew us to them in the first place. Exploring these tensions has long been the subject of my teaching and writing about the western United States, and these essays continue to focus on identifying some of the critical historical, political, ecological, and social contexts that define the many environmental issues that shape life in this vast, and vastly complicated, region; through the writing of these stories I have also been confronted with the need to think a bit more carefully about the various layers of meaning embedded in them.

Some of the chapters, for example, detail policy steps and missteps in public-land management. Others examine the impact of recreation on national forests, parks, and refuges, assess efforts to restore wildland habitat, riparian ecosystems, and endangered species. Others still evaluate the powerful, if contested, role the Antiquities Act, National Environmental Policy Act, and Endangered Species Act play in determining our actions in and reactions to a landscape once dubbed the Trans-Mississippi West.

Consider the contemporary debate over oil and gas drilling adjacent to Chaco Canyon National Historic Park: at a time when "energy independence" is driving the unfettered production everywhere, does this have to include ancient sites that are of inestimable value to Native Americans? Or consider how "local" has become the locale of hope for modern environmentalism: but does this concept mean much without acknowledging that it is every bit as constructed as, say, "bioregionalism"? After all, what we define as local determines how and in what ways we might act in its defense, if defense it needs. Relatedly, placed-based analyses, whatever their geographic scope, need to be rooted in a precise, physical reality. To make a conscientious life in a suburb, floodplain, fire zone, or coastline requires a heightened awareness of these land-scapes' past so that we can develop an intensified sense of responsibility for their present condition and future prospects. Building a more robust sense of justice is essential as well, for that is the key to the creation of more resilient, habitable, and equitable communities.

Sustaining these creative impulses is *Not So Golden State*'s framing device, an insight Aldo Leopold expressed in *A Sand County Almanac*: "All history consists of successive excursions from a single starting point," a location to which "man returns again and again to organize another search for a durable scale of values." This quest, a reflection of the human ambition to know itself in relation to time and space, to organize its energy and structure its insights, is as inevitable as it is unending. That is why the book is mindful of the peripatetic George Caitlin's admonition in *Letters and Notes on the Manners, Customs, Conditions of the North American Indians*: "Few people know the true definition of the term 'West'; and where is its location?— phantomlike it flies before us as we travel, and on our way is continually gilded, before us, as we approach the setting sun." His words beg the question of the region as a distinct environment, and they offer an opportunity to assess the profound influence that such factors as the globalizing of trade across the Pacific have had on the American environmental imagination, then and now.

These more overarching views gain specificity in each of the book's sections. The part titled "Home Turf," for example, explores them through a range of environmental issues confronting the Los Angeles region, not least of which are the links between high country and low, wild and urban. These connections are more obvious in Los Angeles than most places, given its physical geography. The San Gabriel Mountains rise sharply above the valleys below, offering some of the steepest relief on the planet. Cutting through the range's sheer canyons are three major river systems—the Santa Ana, San Gabriel, and Los Angeles—which can carry an astonishing amount of debris that once crashed into low-lying areas with a churning force, but which now are more or less constrained by flood-control dams and channels. Major wildfires, burning with an intensity sparked by annual drought, high heat, and fierce Santa Ana winds, move at lightning speed, smear the air with a thick, acrid smoke, and force thousands to flee. Is it any wonder that critic Mike Davis titled his dystopic analysis of Los Angeles *The Ecology of Fear*?

A fear born of propinquity, of an unexamined closeness to the natural systems that give shape to the varied terrain people inhabit. Not less the air its residents breathe. The city's legendary smog, whose origins lie in its car culture, has been fueled in part by oil that once was locked underneath the region and in the late nineteenth century was brought to the surface, a black-gold rush that powered regional automobility. It also left Angelenos gasping for breath, their eyes stinging: climatic conditions turned exhaust into a toxic ozone layer trapped by the mountains that back in the day were hard to see. Clearing the befouled skies took decades.

Every bit as complex (and partial) has been the enduring effort to regenerate riparian health and restore wildlife habitat in a concrete-hardened landscape. The tensions that have emerged in these initiatives are of a piece with those that thread through the U.S. Forest Service's management of the Angeles National Forest and, not incidentally, emerge whenever a black bear ambles out of the forest and into a nearby subdivision. How we build ourselves into these spaces also depends on the removal of competing users or uses: a historic strawberry patch gives way to a housing development, a memorial forest goes up in smoke, a small creek tells a larger tale of the human impress, and struggles over water—a perennial issue in this oft-dry land—remind us that we are not as free of the past as we would like to think.

"Golden Shore" examines these tensions from the perspective of the California coastline: going whale watching, gazing at sea otters and elephant seals, pondering the ephemeral life of a buckwheat-loving butterfly, or trying to untangle the implications of the human desire to protect endangered flora and fauna makes the shoreline a fraught landscape and a liminal space—and a source of endless stories about the weave of past and present that wash up, like starfish and oyster shells, on beach or rock.

We are as embedded in these marinescapes as we are in terrain that burns: the subject of part 2, "Fiery Terrain." The West does not always flame out every summer; it just seems as if it does. And not every fire is a smoke signal of distress, though many of them are. Picking through the region's fiery terrain is a tricky business, then, as tricky as trying to extinguish a roaring blaze in the baked heat of August. There are lessons to be had by examining how we respond to the seemingly annual conflagrations. The Wallow Fire, which in 2011 burned hundreds of thousands of acres in remote Arizona, sparked a lot of handwringing about wildfire-fighting strategies and an equal amount of political grandstanding. Beyond the headlines and flashy, smoke-filled images lay another reality. The creation of defensible space and the thinning of forest communities, signs of the proactive intervention of homeowners and state and federal agencies, meant that very few structures burned during the month-long Wallow firestorm. That such good news rarely gets reported is part and parcel with another ethical dilemma that too few acknowledge: the decision people make to live in fire zones should come coupled with a recognition of these homeowners' responsibility to do all they can to ensure that their homes do not go up in smoke—how they build their homes and how they landscape their environs are essential steps in defending their space. That obligation comes with another, which was made manifest in the 2013 Yarnell Hill disaster, during which nineteen firefighters lost their lives: to make our houses fire safe is to give the firefighters a fighting chance.

This concept of reciprocity, and the social compact on which it depends, requires us to believe we inhabit common ground with our neighbors and must share space with others—a realization that may help us build a stronger sense of community. That is a tough concept to promote in a bewilderingly antisocial political environment, when budgets for fire prevention are slashed as part of a larger effort to defund the nation-state. Or when the very reasons some people seek to live in isolated, mountainous environs clash with the larger need to act in concert with their communities. Fires illuminate many things, not least the ties that bind and those that are frayed.

"Our Land" develops this argument from a variety of places and perspectives. Most of the chapters revolve around a particular landscape—Gila National Forest, Death Valley, Zion, Arches, and Rocky Mountain National Parks, and a host of other iconic western scenic spots—and asks a series of questions about them: Why do we conceive of wilderness as a preserve, a sanctuary, separate and inviolate? Who benefits (or does not) from the idea that such landscapes are (or ought to be) untrammeled? And why has this intellectual construction, and the preservationist ethos on which it depends, come to dominate contemporary environmentalism? Related queries quickly bubble up after spending time in the newest national park, Pinnacles in Central California, or one of the most venerable, the Grand Canyon in northern Arizona: what impact has the long history of tourism and recreation had on these public lands that we have set aside for these purposes? Maintaining trails that weave through the Yosemite Valley is an arduous, incessant task made more difficult by the volume of visitors that pour into John Muir's favorite terrain or rush to rock climb in Minerva Hoyt's beloved Joshua Tree. Most daunting of all is the prospect of sustained ecological restoration and habitat regeneration under current conditions and those that climate change is generating across the West.

Here again, Leopold can be a trusty guide. That humanity is but "a member of a biotic team is shown by an ecological interpretation of history," he once observed. This being so, it followed that many "historical events, hitherto explained solely in terms of human enterprise, were actually biotic interactions between people and land." Only when "the concept of land as a community really penetrates our intellectual life," will history, as a subject and methodology, become fully realized. My hope is that *Not So Golden State* will contribute in its own way to the realization of this enduring and challenging cross-generational project.

Home Turf

PetroLA

Oil made Southern California—but at a steep price.

It powers the city's modern economy and fuels the region's mobility and its related flow of goods and services. That is evident every time a freight train rumbles out of the Long Beach–Los Angeles ports, among the busiest such complexes on the planet, and heads east to the sprawling Colton rail yard in San Bernardino County. It is clear each day as eighteen-wheelers and cars jam up the 10, 60, and 210 freeways, concrete corridors of carbon monoxide.

Petroleum is also central to the spatial design of greater Los Angeles. Without oil, there would be no freeways, no rail lines, no ports or shipping. Without oil, there would be no suburbs. Without oil, Long Beach would not be Long Beach, or Wilmington, Wilmington.

We do not always see these connections because oil is so tightly woven into every aspect of our lives—from the air we breathe, the food we eat, and the clothes we wear to the gadgets, tools, and toys we buy. This ineluctable connection makes its presence seem invisible, inevitable, unremarkable.

Unless, that is, your home is located near the region's complex transportation grid or one of its major oil fields or refineries. And that is just the infrastructure that is visible: beneath the city runs an underground network of petroleum-carrying pipelines, the densest network under any city, anywhere. That is why in Los Angeles, oil's serious downwind consequences are literally in your face. No surprise, many of these areas are home to some of Southern California's poorest and least advantaged.

Just ask anyone who lives near the ExxonMobil refinery in Torrance. On February 18, 2015, a powerful explosion measuring 1.7 on the Richter scale ripped through the plant, injuring four workers, shattering windows in surrounding neighborhoods, and covering cars, houses, and buses with a thick residue of dust. Children in the fourteen schools that lie within a close radius of the refinery sheltered in place, while panicked parents raced from work and home to make sure their kids were safe. As unsettling as this incident was, it was but one of many incidents that have rattled the community ever since this particular refinery was constructed in 1929.

Telling a similar story are those living close to the Allenco Energy Company's University Park oil wells, near the campus of the University of Southern California (USC). After residents filed hundreds of complaints about headache-inducing odors, nagging respiratory problems, and chronic nosebleeds, in late July 2014 the U.S. Environmental Protection Agency, whose inspectors fell ill when they visited the mismanaged site, fined the company nearly $100,000 for regulatory violations.

At least they got some reaction: by contrast, residents of South Los Angeles have been pressing the Los Angeles City Council for several years to enact stringent regulations on megacorporation Freeport-McMoRan's drilling operations on a site just west of USC. In late January 2016, in angered reaction to the disproportionate attention that city hall paid to a massive gas leak that disrupted life in Porter Ranch, an affluent neighborhood well north of downtown, those living along Jefferson Avenue challenged local politicians and bureaucrats to pay attention to those with less clout and standing. Noted Paul Parks, head of the Redeemer Community Partnership: "How does the Planning Department hear all these health and safety concerns—and then just walk away as if it never happened?"

The same question has been asked by those living adjacent to the Inglewood oil field (the largest in Los Angeles County) and those around the Brea-Olinda site (the most productive in Orange County). They are convinced that hydraulic fracturing (or "fracking") is negatively impacting air and water quality, a conviction intensified when in early 2015 state data revealed that extremely high levels of benzene, toluene, and chromium-6 have been detected in fracking waste wells across the state—several *thousand* times higher than those the California Office of Environmental Health Hazard Assessment has established as acceptable. Since then, grassroots organizations in such communities as La Habra Heights, Baldwin Hills, and Whittier have been pressuring public officials to ban or at least heavily regulate this controversial technique of well stimulation. In Hermosa Beach, a spring 2015 ballot initiative that would have allowed new wells to be drilled in the heart of the tourist-packed coastal community was roundly defeated.

There is nothing new about these protests in Southern California: the close connection between energy production, the integrity of residential neighborhoods, and community health has been a hot-button issue since the first black-gold strike in the region in 1892. Indeed, this tight link between past and present, between the historical debates over and contemporary struggles to resolve Southern California's century-long dependence on fossil fuels, and the troubling consequences that this dependency has produced, is threaded into the built environment and the human experience of it.

Those consequences were manifest from the moment speculators first drilled into LA's streetscape, punched holes in its parks, and built derricks along every square foot of beachfront. Even as many early twentieth-century Angelenos scrambled to take advantage of this oil boom, others, who also benefited from the rush, battled against the industry's unregulated expansion into their subdivisions. Their complicity in the very thing that they steadfastly opposed is one reason historian Nancy Quam-Wickham describes that era's opposition as emblematic of Los Angeles's "uneasy relationship with petroleum."

That relationship grew ever more complicated during World War II. Southern Californians were as patriotic as the next American, but when oil companies wrapped themselves in the flag to secure political support for their mad-dash pumping of all crude under their homes, and regardless of location and whoever was displaced by their actions, some citizens and politicians fought back against what one decried as a "wildcat oil scheme." The federal government entered the fray and squashed attempts to regulate oil production in Southern California; as historian Sarah Elkind has observed, such a "national emergency can undermine local legal protections that the community has agreed upon, and can erode local government's ability to control powerful interests." That said, it remains telling that even wartime emergencies did not silence all critics of unrestrained pumping.

Peacetime brought prosperity that fueled a more aggressive anti-petro movement. Witness what happened in late January 1969 when Union Oil's offshore Platform A blew out just off the Santa Barbara coast. The resulting 100,000-barrel spill, at the time the largest in U.S. history, devastated wildlife populations, blackened beaches, and infuriated the public. The backlash went national, intensified in part by the publication of the Santa Barbara Declaration of Environmental Rights. Its author, Roderick Frazier Nash, offered a powerful challenge to the fossil-fuel industry's unchecked clout: "We must develop a vision to see that in regard to the natural world private and corporate ownership should be so limited as to preserve the interest of society and the integrity of the environment."

Nash's galvanizing words were at the heart of other struggles to control tailpipe and smokestack emissions then fouling the regional airshed. So poisonous could it become that schoolchildren were kept indoors, adults commuting to work could be seen wearing gas masks, and the San Gabriel Mountains, the tallest peak of which towers 10,000 feet above Los Angeles, disappeared from view; the City of Angels became Smogtown. To clear the air, local activists found that they had to fight against a recalcitrant city hall, battle with a resistant state house, and take on a stonewalling automobile industry; convincing these members of the power elite required decades of organized opposition. Their efforts bore some fruit: the establishment of effective air quality management districts across the Golden State is one example; the fact that Angelenos can now see the San Gabriel Mountains is another. However improved, Southern California continues to have some of the nation's worst air quality, a direct ramification of what landscape designer Kate Orff argues in *Petrochemical America* about the foundational elements of the nation's built landscape; by design, it is "a machine for consuming oil and gas."

New energy sources—or, rather, old sources reenergized—add to the dilemmas confronting the Southland in the first decades of the twenty-first century. Hydraulic fracturing technologies and acidization of oil and gas wells have created new threats to groundwater and air quality. To fight against these hazards, national organizations such as the Natural Resources Defense Council (NRDC) have joined with neighborhood associations and local environmental organizations to challenge production in the region's oil fields. Residents of Baldwin Hills and Culver City, whose homes abut the Inglewood oil field, like those in Fullerton and Whittier, whose homes are sited close to the Brea-Olinda field, and those living close to Santa Barbara County's pumps and derricks, are pressuring government officials to step up. These campaigns, and such state regulatory initiatives, make a larger point, too. Protecting one's home ground and physical health is intimately connected to larger concerns about global climate disruption that our heavy use of fossil fuels—and the resulting carbon economy—is accelerating.

This framing of the debate also flips on its head the argument an early Los Angeles oil wildcatter advanced in support of the "smoke, noise, and dirt" his industry produced, which he deemed essential "to the growth, expansion, and upbuilding of our beautiful city." Heeding oil's many critics, he declared, would turn "our city of the living . . . into a veritable city of the dead."

We now know the opposite is true.

Air Apparent

The act of breathing is pretty straightforward, and when everything is functioning properly, it is an unconscious, autonomic response. Yet the chemical composition of the air we are breathing is not so clear-cut, which means we need to be intensely aware of what we are inhaling (and at what time of day we are drawing this essential oxygen into our lungs).

Angelenos have been sensitive to this dilemma for some time. In the 1920s, when more than 430,000 cars were registered in Los Angeles (a 1:3 ratio; today, it is roughly 1:1), the region's residents began to recognize that their Ford Model Ts, Pierce-Arrow Runabouts, and Cadillac Coupes were befouling the air.

No one could have any doubt about this toxic consequence by the 1940s: a thick dark layer of smog blanketed the basin. Yes, there were deniers, which Detroit auto manufacturers paid well to cloud the issue, but in retrospect we know they were dead wrong. The sky didn't lie.

Yet its relative clarity in the early twenty-first century—residents can actually see the surrounding mountains and hills that but thirty years ago were muffled in a brown smear—is also to a degree misleading. That is the troubling news embedded in the American Lung Association's (ALA) 2015 "State of the Air" report.

First the upbeat evidence: California in general and the Southland in particular have experienced fewer ozone alerts than occurred in 2000; in LA that amounted to nearly twenty-four more healthful days. The overall levels of pollution moreover are also lower than they were at the beginning of this century.

But however feel-good this data may be, air quality in Los Angeles still does not get a passing grade: it receives an F for levels of ozone and for twenty-four-hour and annual rates of particle pollution. "If you live in Los Angeles County," the ALA announces in the guarded language of science, "the air you breathe may put your health at risk."

The organization says the same thing about virtually every urban county in California, each of which, from San Diego and Riverside to Santa Barbara, Santa Clara, and Alameda, earns a solid F. Flunking, too, are the Big Ag counties of the San Joaquin and Central Valleys and their peers to the south, such as the Imperial Valley; any place downwind of their exhaust-spewing, dust-spiraling, and fertilizer-laced operations also was downgraded.

Only San Francisco received a gold star on its report card. Subtracting those living in the City by the Bay and similarly salubrious climes—some coastal, others mountainous—left an estimated 90 percent of Californians breathing a lot of bad air. Its poor quality is compromising our lungs and impairing our collective health.

Some suffer more than others. Those living around oil refineries in El Segundo and Richmond, for example, bear a greater burden than do those residing upwind or at some remove from these plants' airborne toxins. Inhabitants of mountainous Placer and Nevada Counties have the bad luck to inhale wind-driven pollution from industrialized agriculture in the lowlands below. Residents of the sprawling Inland Empire suffer from local auto emissions but even more from those that the stiff westerlies drive east every afternoon to pile up against the San Gabriel and San Bernardino Mountains; what happens on the west side of Los Angeles does not stay there.

These environmental injustices are compounded in Los Angeles, especially when set within the regional freeway grid.

Start with the fact that these high-speed roadways, and their multistacked interchanges, were blasted through or pounded into some of the city's most underprivileged, economically distressed, and politically disenfranchised neighborhoods and barrios. These communities' public health was sacrificed so that a generally better-heeled population could zoom overhead.

This harmful history comes with a cautionary health warning. Until very recently the maxim was that if you lived within 1,000 feet of any of the highways that slice through Watts, Compton, or the Eastside (or crisscross the valley floors), your odds of breathing poor air is higher than those who lived farther away from, say, the 5, 10, 60, or 101 freeways.

Now we learn that the pollution plume streaming out of auto tailpipes and eighteen-wheeler exhaust stacks is more dangerous to more people because it is far more mobile and penetrating than previously thought. Researchers at UCLA and the California Air Resources Board made this discovery when they tracked the flow of emissions that billows up from LA's dense grid of high-speed highways.

Using a zero-emission vehicle mounted with an array of sensitive instruments to measure ultrafine particles and calculate the presence of those bad boys of air pollution—carbon monoxide and nitric oxide—they drove along surface streets that run perpendicular to a series of heavily trafficked freeways. Rather than do so during peak rush hours, morning and afternoon, they selected 4:30 to 6:30 a.m. as their time frame.

The results, published in a 2012 issue of *Atmospheric Environment*, are distressing. The early morning hours prove critical to the spread of a toxic cloud that can extend a mile or more from the source, upwards of five times farther than had been believed to be the case.

More unsettling, this pollution has the capacity to infiltrate homes at that distance as well. "Although closed windows help block the particles from seeping inside, previous studies have shown that indoor pollution levels still reach 50 to 70 percent of outdoor levels," researchers noted. Within the newly broadened impact zone, Angelenos cannot avoid inhaling these toxins even as we slumber.

"This is happening around every freeway," says project head Suzanne Paulson of UCLA's Department of Atmospheric and Oceanic Sciences and the Institute of the Environment and Sustainability, "and a similar situation likely happens around the world in the early morning hours. The particles tend to end up indoors, so a lot of people are being exposed inside their homes and schools."

Should those predawn hours be an Angeleno's preferred time to exercise in the Great Outdoors, she or he might want to reconsider. In Southern California the typical overnight cooling leads to what is called a nocturnal surface inversion: it traps freeway-generated pollution close to the ground, and then breezes move the concentrated soup downwind. This "nocturnal boundary layer" does not decay until after the sun rises, the atmosphere heats, and the winds kick up, mixing this unhealthy low-lying plume with cleaner air above.

If your aerobic regime and route takes you into the noxious zone, whose durability is more pronounced in the dark mornings of winter than in sun-kissed summer morns, you are increasing your risks of an array of health-related problems. For adults that could include asthma, heart disease, and strokes; for children it might mean preterm births, low birth weights, and diabetes.

Given that an estimated 25 percent of the South-land's population lives within this danger zone, millions are directly affected.

I'm among them. Our home in Claremont lies right within the area of greatest impact, a mile south of the car-clogged 210 freeway. Worse, the self-described City of Trees was one of the researchers' testing sites, and their analysis of its geographical siting suggests it is particularly vulnerable to drifting pollution. The early morning air flow at the overpass of Mountain Avenue and the 210 is "the least variable [in the study] due to the adjacent [San Gabriel] mountains to the north which produce a strong, thermally-induced, mountain-valley wind system."

Ruh-roh.

What I have loved most about my predawn, quick-paced treks is pushing up that very same sloping avenue into the face of the cool northerly breeze, with the dark foothills and rim-lit mountains guiding me up the now-concretized alluvial fan. My daily routine, which has seemed so heart strengthening, energy boosting, and resilience building, may have been undercutting those presumed beneficial outcomes.

It almost makes me want to stop breathing.

Razed Expectations

In December 2012, the U.S. Army Corps of Engineers did what it often does best—it disappointed. With little public notice, the Corps gutted more than forty acres of thick vegetation along Haskell Creek as it flows through the Sepulveda Basin before emptying into the LA River. Did the Corps believe that no one would care? Or, that even if people came upon its hack job, the traumatized terrain would elicit no comment? Or did the agency simply decide to act as it so often has in the past, with little regard to the environmental consequences, and the public be damned?

One of those convinced that the Corps had been blinded by the dazzling allure of its technical expertise is Kris Ohlenkamp, former president of the San Fernando Valley Audubon Society. He was among a group who stumbled upon the bulldozed landscape during that year's annual Christmas Bird Count, and he decried the federal agency's retrogressive actions: "This is the old Corps of the '50s and '60s that destroyed the Everglades," he told a local radio station; "they've promised to get away from that."

This particular vow went unfulfilled. The Corps's unilateral decision to chop down mature cottonwoods and willows, bury Pothole Pond and its wetland habitat, and rip out understory plants and grasses within the basin undercuts its professed change in behavior: "They've said it's a mandate of the Corps to be good stewards of the environment and assure a diversity of habitats," Ohlenkamp asserted, but after wandering through the blunt-cut vegetation he remained unconvinced.

The agency's initial response to the resulting outcry did not help matters: "Somehow, we did not clearly communicate" with local environmental and neighborhood groups, Army Corps Deputy District Commander Alexander Deraney acknowledged to the *Los Angeles Times*. He swore the Corps would "make the process more transparent in the future."

For local activists and lovers of the once-fecund terrain, none of his words gave confidence that the agency had in fact learned from its less-than-pristine history or that its much-heralded (and greener) future will ever arrive.

In the Corps's defense, the land in question has been heavily manipulated since the early 1940s. Part of the vast flood-control system that has restructured the entire length of the Los Angeles River watershed, it lies to the west of nearby Sepulveda Dam, which was constructed in 1941. The earth-filled embankment and its iconic gated spillway are the pivot around which much of

Los Angeles revolves: the dam has protected downstream neighborhoods (and allowed others to be built). The postwar concretization of the upstream riverbed allowed the development of an autocentric San Fernando Valley, and to serve this booming suburban population, a sprawling recreation area has evolved within the basin itself. Seen from the sky, the Sepulveda Dam gives dramatic contour to the regional flow of people and water. Nothing about it and its environs seems natural, unmanaged.

Yet that is precisely why people were so upset by the Corps's marauding through acreage that contained the ecological building blocks of much-needed riparian habitat. Since the 1980s, and with express permission and financial support from the relevant public agencies, volunteers have been planting elderberry, willows, coyote brush, and other indigenous plant material as part of a restoration initiative that has (or had) taken on a life of its own. Tall trees with a thick understory, water flowing and still, and a range of open and densely vegetated space—innumerable species had come to call this zone home.

They did, too, especially birds. Indeed, determining their presence is precisely why the San Fernando Audubon Society, like its peer groups around the world, mounts the annual Christmas Bird Count. The Audubon Society established the first such in 1900 when it was itself a fledgling organization. Frank Chapman, one of its founding ornithologists, promoted the idea as a beneficial counter to the Yuletide tradition of indiscriminate and competitive gunning down of birds.

Ever since, the concept has taken flight, as families and friends tabulate resident and migratory avian populations, building up what Chapman had called "a census of Christmas bird-life." For more than a century, these citizen scientists have compiled a wealth of data that has deepened our ecological understanding of the interaction between birds and the landscapes that sustain them.

It is just such diligent activism that has helped us know definitively that Sepulveda Basin supports robust, year-round populations of a range of birds—great and snowy egrets, night-crowned and green herons, turkey vultures, ring-billed gulls, and greater white-fronted geese, as well as all manner of doves and pigeons, warblers, finches, and wrens, ducks and hawks. Sharp-eyed birders have enumerated year after year that the site is as well a critical way station for those species flying in for a portion of the winter, among them the common moorhen, Virginia rail, Nuttall's woodpecker, and lesser yellowlegs; eagles (golden and bald), peregrine falcons, and chipping sparrows. The creekside acres, brutalized by what the local Audubon Society likened to "a mechanized blitzkrieg assault," were very much alive.

Their vibrancy is why the Corps's declaration that it did not need to file an environmental impact statement because there was nothing on the ground to impact was so galling. Although the agency conceded that some birds flew overhead now and again, and that there was the odd squirrel nosing about, it argued that otherwise the area was devoid of significance; by its calculation, there was no species or habitat worth identifying or protecting.

The agency's casual dismissal was born in part of its monomaniacal focus on its perceived mission—the Sepulveda Basin is designed as flood-control infrastructure, and nothing should interfere with its proper functioning. It was also a consequence of the George W. Bush administration's willingness to cut federal land managers a lot of slack in terms of how they interpreted environmental regulations. The Bush White House did so in hopes of foiling the people's ability to challenge agencies' actions in court, rights hitherto protected under the National Environmental Policy Act of 1970 and repeatedly affirmed in one lawsuit after another. Yet those who advocated clear-cutting forests, mowing down grasslands, drilling or fracking the public lands without restraint, and building dams and levees had little interest in public oversight. The Bush administration gave them their lead; its successor did not entirely rein them in, either. What happened to this relatively small plot of land in Southern California is happening across the country.

Like those elsewhere, people here were infuriated. Scathing critiques online, damning newspaper stories, and exposés in the electronic media forced the Corps to call a temporary halt to its "Vegetation Management Project." It agreed to meet with some of the aggrieved parties, notably the whistle-blowing San Fernando Audubon Society, and to clue them in on its long-term plans. Skeptics abounded. One of them, state senator Kevin de Leon (D–Los Angeles), was among a number of local politicians who went public with their demands for clarification. "When a clunky federal bureaucracy doesn't collaborate with state and local officials and community leaders," de Leon asserted in the *Los Angeles Times*, "you create a real mess, which is what we have right now in the Sepulveda Basin."

Two years later, the Corps had not cleaned up the messed-up environment, and it is easy to see why not: as my students and I walked through the affected area, baking in the late August heat without a shade tree in sight, it became clear just how thoroughly it had devastated the formerly healthy terrain; the land was flattened, plant material and debris swept away, and after spraying herbicides to kill off unwanted regeneration, the Corps had planted acres of non-native saw grass.

It is impossible to imagine that the Corps's construction of this sterile monoculture, so consistent with its concrete fixation, will ever come close to matching the rich biota that citizen-led restoration efforts had nurtured and attracted to the site. Like a wolf peeing on its territorial boundaries, the U.S. Army Corps of Engineers, with bulldozer and chainsaw, had marked its turf, and the result was a scandalous diminishing of nature and democracy.

Wading in the Water

I thought I knew what to expect when my students and I went down to the river. After all, we had read Blake Gumprecht's compelling *Los Angeles River: Its Life, Death, and Possible Rebirth*. We had dug into Norris Hundley's encyclopedic *The Great Thirst* and were jolted by environmental historian Jenny Price's lyrical essay "Thirteen Ways of Seeing Nature in L.A."

These master narrators of the fifty-two-mile-long Los Angeles River frame its past condition and contemporary state in ways as interwoven as the river's threaded course once was as it flowed down the San Fernando Valley, pressed through the Glendale Narrows, and then fanned out across the LA Basin on its way to the sea.

Through differing lenses, Hundley and Gumprecht focus on the complicated ways those who have resided along the river have responded to its periods of dry and wet. The arid months were much less dangerous, of course. But the thunderous winter floods that could swiftly crash over or blow through the river's banks, and pummel the surrounding built environment, were properly feared.

Or at least that was the reaction of the region's Euro-American colonists: they were more flat-footed than the seasonally savvy and mobile native peoples, who knew where not to live in a time of heavy rain.

Those floodwaters posed another dilemma for those who planted themselves so firmly within the river's watershed—the floods' sediment-packed, scouring energy ("damaging debris discharges" is what the LA Department of Public Works calls this process) could churn new paths to a new mouth.

This volatility and variability is hard to appreciate today, as the river follows a concrete-fixed course out of the downtown area, on a relatively straight shot before it pours into San Pedro Bay, near Long Beach. Prior to being boxed in, however, the LA River streamed into the Pacific anywhere between San Pedro and Santa Monica Bays, an unpredictability that drove real estate developers, civic leaders, and flood-weary residents crazy.

They went a little vengeful-crazy following the blockbuster 1938 floods, which pounded the Southland, killing more than one hundred people, wiping out earthen levees, and ripping through neighborhoods and commercial districts. A quick-setting political consensus drove the call for the U.S. Army Corps of Engineers and the LA County Flood Control District to do what they do most—pour concrete (Gumprecht estimates that upwards of 3.5 million barrels went into the reconstruction of the river by the late 1950s).

In a post-Katrina age, it is inevitable as well that we might doubt the knee-jerk reaction to make rigid what had been a flexible natural system. But in the late 1930s and early 1940s, and well into the next decade, there were few naysayers as the Corps and district laid down cubic yard after cubic yard into the construction of upstream dams (Hansen, Sepulveda, and Big Tujunga, among others). Full channelization of the river's banks and the construction of countless culverts and storm drains helped capture and flush water into a river that now largely functioned as a flood-control device for its 834-square-mile watershed. We had formed up nature to our liking.

That structural reconfiguration was what my students and I anticipated seeing when we rendezvoused at Steelhead Park, just off Riverside Drive in the Glendale Narrows. We weren't disappointed.

This pocket park, one of several designed to open up some greenspace along the river's hardened course, demarcates the southerly end of a short stretch of soft-bottom riverbed. The hard-wall, steep-slanted banks and the fully concretized channel that runs south beneath the Figueroa Street Bridge make it an ideal spot to consider the confluence of social and natural forces that define this space.

Helping us think about some of these tensions was Peter Enzminger. He had taken the first iteration of my class Water in the West in spring 2008, and was finishing up his master's in urban planning at USC. As part of his studies, Peter developed a model for how during the summer people could make more use of the hardened river bottom itself. His goal was to draw them off the bike/walk path that runs along the bank to deepen their connection to the river as a river. I asked him to share his insights with us, and as we sat in the small amphitheater-like seating at the park, he located his project within the larger effort to revitalize the river.

Dating from the quixotic founding of the Friends of the LA River (FOLAR) in 1985, whose idealistic enthusiasm has pushed public dialogue to such a point that we now have a fully developed river revitalization plan, the goal has been to elevate Angelenos' consciousness about the watershed they inhabit.

Seeing the river afresh initially required cutting through the chain-link that fenced it off from the curious; it also required punching holes in the hard-and-fast politics of flood control that dominated civic conversations about the LA River's place in the community.

Over the years and as a result of countless local hearings, neighborhood confabs, and planning charrettes, a new politics about the river started to emerge that reflected FOLAR's grand ambitions of the mid-1980s. It had a singular focus, asserted one of its cofounders, poet Lewis MacAdams, in the *Whole Earth Review*: to run the river from an "urban hell" into "a sylvan glen, a thicket, an avalon, a marsh, a place of great blue herons, where a kingfisher darting at a steelhead's flash might accidentally flush a doe."

Peter's playful project—employing wooden pallets to make a platform on the river bottom that can be moved around like puzzle pieces during the dry months and serve as an informal gathering spot, and then forklifted out during the wet ones—fit within this larger ethos that conceives of the river as a living resource and communal responsibility.

Before pedaling away to sketch out new ideas upstream, Peter brought us back to the river's current structure and the cavernous space it created; its vastness, its monumentality is overwhelming, he said.

He was right. When we walked down the embankment and into the riverbed, and positioned ourselves directly beneath the Figueroa Bridge, everything appeared out of scale. The sheer-walled channel conveyed something of the magnitude of the engineering project, and its depth and width (roughly 50 by 200 feet) bespoke the sheer volume of water that could sluice full speed through this site on its way to the Pacific; it's been clocked at 45 miles an hour. The flood-controllers' ambition was outsized.

It also remains palpable. As struck as we were by the geometric angularity of the space—its bed, wall, and bridges—and by the energy and transportation grids that arc overhead and by the muffled hum of cars and the screech of Metrolink brakes, running beneath this urban dynamic was another pulse, small, unmistakable, and surprising.

The river was animated.

Some of this had to do with the fact that we were there but two days after heavy rains, so there was a good flow slipping across the concrete. Some had to do with the bobbing presence of a clutch of black-necked stilts feeding in the waters just south of the natural-bottom narrows; same with a pair of mallards wriggling through a tangle of root and trunk.

More consequential, I think, was how—and sneakily so—the river came alive for us as we stood in its gurgling midst. "I did not expect the inner channel," Jess, a student, later reflected. "Of all the things that I saw last Tuesday, I don't know why that inner, two-foot-deep channel full of water rushing along made the biggest impression, but it did."

Certain in advance that it would not "feel like a real river," she came to realize that the "inner channel gave it life." In its rush, "the currents played, swirling the water and creating my favorite sounds, as it hurried off downstream. The river seemed alive because it did not behave perfectly—water from the inner channel sloshed out, soaking the rest of the riverbed in a few inches of water and allowing the algae to grow even on the concrete."

Jenny Price taught us to look for markers like that: to see nature in the cracks, like the six-inch waterfall the river has been making as it slowly undercuts the seam between two concrete slabs, a tiny cataract that, if you stood still, roared. I took that as an instance, however microscopic, of what Price asserts: "Nature is never passive."

Because every place "has an active, very particular ecology, climate, topography, geology, flora, fauna," the task is to locate its constituent elements, peculiar and prosaic, and to write about them, dream about them, affirm them. "What we need in L.A., as elsewhere," Price has written, "is a foundational literature that imagines nature not as the opposite of the city but as the basic stuff of modern everyday life."

The Los Angeles River is that wellspring for Price, and it became so for another of my students, who was initially repelled by it: "The river is a hodge-podge of cement that looks like sand, trash that looks like trees, and life that is so surrounded by the city that you feel like you need to poke it to make sure it's alive." So Kristen wrote, but her critical perspective shifted as she headed down the steep, concretized bank: "From the bottom up, it's hard to forget that it's enormous and moving, and as I experienced it, it seemed to regain some of the life that its ugly urbanization had taken from it."

Then a childhood memory surfaced, of hours spent in the concrete-lined irrigation ditch that runs behind her Boulder, Colorado, backyard. It's "a place where I could see snails and moss peeling in the fall and chase water spiders that didn't know. I was cherishing the river as a form of Jenny Price's urban nature, a form which I saw as both beautiful and alive."

The prospects are beguilingly complex: "When we begin to believe, as I did when I was young," Kristen wrote, that "our rivers, even our artificial rivers, are magic, we allow ourselves to care about them, and in doing so we give them potential, a potential which, while painful, can also be liberating."

I did not see that coming, either.

Landmark Mountains

The San Gabriel Mountains are Southern California's spectacular foreground and dramatic backdrop; they occupy a pivotal place in the Southern Californian imagination, past and present. On October 10, 2014, a sun-drenched and smoggy day, President Barack Obama underscored their local centrality when he used the executive authority granted to him by the Antiquities Act of 1906 to designate a portion of the Angeles National Forest as the San Gabriel Mountains National Monument.

To its promoters, the switch in nomenclature was critical. They believe that the nearly 350,000-acre national monument will generate additional dollars that will enable the U.S. Forest Service to enhance the visitor experience. That it needed enhancing was without doubt. Trees and rock faces have been tagged, and trash has been strewn across meadows, scenic areas, and riverbanks; sodden diapers clogging the east and west fork of the San Gabriel River, whose headwaters lie within this rugged mountain range, are a too common sight. Pomona College geologist Jade Star Lackey once likened this devastation to a desecration. "On field trips we commonly go off the beaten path in search of outcrops, only to find ravines filled with trash and bullet-riddled appliances," Lackey told the *Student Life*, the newspaper of record for the Claremont Colleges (institutions that routinely use images of the snow-capped San Gabriels for admissions brochures and press releases). "We often pull up to a favorite outcrop that we've used for years to teach important geologic concepts like cross-cutting relations, only to find that it's covered with graffiti."

Cleaning up this distressed landscape has been and will continue to be costly. The prospect of a relatively robust stream of federal dollars, always an iffy proposition, became even more so after the 2014 midterm elections, in which the Republican Party captured the U.S. Senate and House. In this parsimonious context and polarized environment, the entire system of public lands in the United States—national forests, parks, grasslands, and refuges—goes begging.

There may be some relief from the private sector, with an increase in philanthropic dollars. In conjunction with the president's designation, for example, the National Forest Foundation (NFF) announced the creation of a new $3 million fund for the San Gabriel National Monument. Since the 2009 Station Fire, which torched more than 160,000 acres in the Angeles National Forest, the NFF has been active in underwriting restoration projects in one of the worst-hit areas, including Big Tujunga Canyon and other burned-over sites now located within the national monument. The goal then was to rehabilitate damaged riparian corridors and replant the headwaters to protect against erosion and boost the forest's capacity to sequester carbon, while rebuilding recreational opportunities in the forest.

That work is ongoing, but the NFF, which Congress chartered in 1990 to support the Forest Service's land-management efforts, has taken on a new role with the new designation. Its San Gabriel fund has helped jump-start rehabilitation of those acres most battered by the annual influx of more than 3 million visitors. "This designation provides an exciting opportunity for the Forest Service and Los Angeles's business and civic communities to provide residents and visitors with improved conditions to enjoy their public lands," observed NFF president Bill Possiel at the time. The fund will deepen "our commitment to long-term stewardship with community-based partners and to connecting Los Angeles County's diverse residents to the National Monument."

That social good has been difficult to achieve, however, given that the monument, for all its size, is not as large or as comprehensive as originally intended. The first iteration called for it to absorb the whole of the San Gabriel range, stretching from the Cajon Pass on the east (through which I-15 cuts) to Newhall Pass on the west (through which CA-14 runs, connecting the Mojave Desert to the Los Angeles Basin). The logic was driven by geographic realities and management needs. By absorbing the entire Angeles National Forest and that portion of the range that the San Bernardino National Forest stewards, the national monument would streamline administration, making for more efficient and effective governance.

That plan made perfect sense on paper, but failed to gain traction in the less-than-perfect political arena. Supervisors of San Bernardino County, for example, responding to mountain communities such as Mount Baldy Village and Wrightwood opposed to what some there decried as a "federal land grab," unanimously opposed the designation: the irony is delicious, given that by definition a national forest is federal. The Obama administration responded by shrinking the monument so that its eastern boundary runs in tandem with the Los Angeles–San Bernardino County line. However understandable the decision to limit the monument's size may have been, it has hampered efforts to manage recreation, wilderness, and endangered species in a more unified fashion.

Those managerial efforts have been further complicated by the troubling fact that the San Gabriel Mountains National Monument does not include all of the Angeles National Forest, either. Even as the Forest Service developed an administrative structure that nested the monument within the Angeles National Forest's supervisory flow chart, the inevitable overlapping authorities have not brought clarity to decision-making processes or streamlined procedures, which is one of the issues that the monument's proponents had hoped to resolve through the original designation.

None of these difficulties—potential and predict-able—undercuts the San Gabriels' claim to national monument status, as defined by the Antiquities Act. The legislators who conceived of the act in the early twentieth century identified a set of qualities needed to secure national monument status, among them historic landmarks, historic and prehistoric structures, and other objects of historic or scientific interest that are situated on the lands owned or controlled by the government of the United States. These mountains more than meet this benchmark for reasons natural and human, not all of which are benign.

"The San Gabriels, in their state of tectonic youth, are rising as rapidly as any range on earth," John McPhee observed in *The Control of Nature.* "Their loose inimical slopes flout the tolerance of the angle of repose. Rising straight up out of the megalopolis, they stand 10,000 feet above the nearby sea, and they are not kidding with this city. Shedding, spalling, self-destructing, they are disinte-grating at a rate that is also among the fastest in the world. The phalanxed communities of Los Angeles have pushed themselves hard against these mountains, an aggression that requires a deep defense budget to contend with the results."

The very dangers of uplift and sloughing off add to this range's uniqueness: when rain falls on their loose soils, the resulting debris flows are beyond treacherous; a freak monsoonal storm in August 2014 dropped four inches of rain on the Mount Baldy watershed, setting loose a churning torrent of rock, gravel, trees, and soil that killed one man, smashed houses, buried automobiles, and gouged out roads. This same terrain, under scorching sun and fanned by furious Santa Ana winds, can funnel firestorms down slope and through canyon to incinerate broad swaths of these stiff-folded mountains. Fascinating and terrifying, the San Gabriels are one of a kind.

They are home as well to some unusual geological features—the shape-shifting San Andreas Fault, for one—and a rich biodiversity consistent with Mediterranean ecozones that cover but 3 percent of the earth's surface. More than 80 percent of the forest is covered in chaparral (a "bristly mane" is how John Muir described it after hiking there in the 1870s), a habitat that contains upwards of three hundred species of plants endemic to this region. Its streams, creeks, and springs sustain such threatened or endangered species as the yellow-legged frog and arroyo chub, while Nelson's bighorn sheep occupy portions of the mountains' windswept high ground; sailing high overhead are California condors.

These distinguishing features are matched by the mountains' remarkable human history, which dates back 12,000 years. Native people used the foothills, ridges, and canyons for food, clothing, and shelter. They hunted across the rough land, made use of its pristine waters, and set fires, one historian has written, to "enhance the density of specific edible plant communities, increase the food supply for animals, and support the development of material used in construction and medicine." Central to indigenous cosmology, the San Gabriel Mountains were also these communities' source of life.

The San Gabriels proved as rich for the Europeans; ranching and agriculture made use of rain and snowmelt that flowed downhill. There would have been no citrus production in Southern California without these remarkable mountains and the alluvial fans that spread out from their canyons. The same can be said for recreation. The San Gabriels were the stimulus to the so-called Great Hiking Era of the late nineteenth and early twentieth centuries. Hundreds of thousands of Angelenos took streetcars to trailheads in the foothills, then trekked up Mount Wilson and Mount Baldy, and slept in the high country lodges that catered to their needs, blazing a trail for the more than 3 million people today who splash in the San Gabriel River, rest within a shady oak grove, or venture into the Sheep Mountain Wilderness.

We can continue to commune with nature whether this place is called the Angeles National Forest or the San Gabriel Mountains National Monument. And maybe that's the point: the lands are more important than any name we bestow on them. Yet their new status as a national monument perhaps offers us an unparalleled opportunity in this climate-changed era to repair this rugged environment so that it will do what it has always done—sustain the human and biotic communities that depend on them.

Arboreal Panacea

I have nothing against trees. Love them, in fact—their bark: rough, smooth, or grooved; their needles or leaves: angular, flat, jagged, or pointed; branches crooked or straight; roots gnarled. I'll forbear quoting Joyce Kilmer about how lovely trees can be (but you hear that poetic ditty in your head, don't you?) and will just confess that I'm a big fan of the arboreal.

A more scientific catalog of their virtues appeared in an April 2012 issue of the *New York Times*, penned by Jim Robbins, author of *The Man Who Planted Trees*. Central to Robbins's claims for why trees matter is the positive role they can play in sustaining public health.

He observes not surprisingly that trees are quite efficient water filters. They are "capable of cleaning up the most toxic wastes, including explosives, solvents and organic wastes," he writes, and do so "largely through a dense community of microbes around the tree's roots that clean water in exchange for nutrients, a process known as phytoremediation."

Because of their remarkable—their life-essential—task of converting carbon dioxide into organic compounds such as sugar and then releasing oxygen (their waste, our gain), trees have the unusual ability to cleanse the air we breathe.

By themselves, they cannot compensate for all the toxins that blow out of the tailpipes, smokestacks, or cooling towers in Los Angeles or Houston, cities with some of the nation's dirtiest air. Yet at a more micro level, such as a street block, their leafy presence has been linked to the reduction of asthma.

Like a host of foresters and urban planners, Robbins is convinced that trees form a kind of green shield. Their canopy as forests, and as cover along streets, can cool soil and concrete, decreasing temperatures and moderating heat-island effects. By releasing an aerosol mist (forest bathing, the Japanese call it), they can make life more bearable for any species inhabiting these particular landscapes.

But can they help humanity adapt to and mitigate the immensity of climate change? That they can sequester carbon has been much touted in policymaking circles as one tool to help shrink our carbon footprint; and thus trees seem critical to the larger effort to reduce global warming.

Yet it does not necessarily follow, as Robbins and others assume, that we must reforest the planet as rapidly as possible. Robbins's motivation for this conclusion comes through his citing of a much-loved Chinese aphorism: "'When is the best time to plant a tree?' The answer: 'Twenty years ago. The second-best time? Today.'"

That's where I balk. If we had a more complete picture of the variations of potential temperature change across ecosystems and topographies; if we could pinpoint when and where alterations in precipitation will occur; and if we were we able to calibrate the shifting influence that heat, light, and wet will have on differing soil types, then we might have a clue about what tree species to plant in which biota and at what times.

But we don't. So to plant trees in hopes that they will survive, and thus increase our odds of doing so, seems, at best, random.

Consider what happened in the scorched aftermath of the 2009 Station Fire that torched 250 square miles of the San Gabriels. Fearful that the erosive force of winter rainy seasons would strip the burned-over district of its soil, the Forest Service mounted an aggressive restoration project. Beginning in April 2011, contract labor planted 1 million seedlings; another 2 million were to have been planted over the next five years. The goal was to regreen approximately 11,000 acres of the 160,000 that the fire had consumed.

Such ambitions outran reality. Only about 25 percent of the seedlings dug into charred slopes, cindered meadows, and blackened canyon floors survived the first year, a 75 percent mortality rate that stunned agency foresters. "When we planted seedlings, conditions were ideal in terms of soil composition and temperature, rainfall and weather trends," one of them told the *Los Angeles*

Times. "Then the ground dried out and there just wasn't enough moisture after we planted."

The Forest Service had to go back to the drawing board, shrinking the number of acres to be planted and, where possible, switching to tree species that are indigenous to the San Gabriel Mountains.

Critics are unappeased. One of them is ecologist Richard Halsey, director of the California Chaparral Institute. His initial skepticism of the project had led him to lambaste the choice of Coulter pine, a nonnative tree, as the keystone tree in the regenerative mix. The news of the subsequent die-off came as no surprise: "The reality we live in is a Mediterranean climate, and there is just not enough water to create what they have in mind. I do not believe they will succeed because this is Southern California, not rain-drenched Oregon."

This climatic reality is part of the reason there has been a very long history of flawed regeneration projects on county and federal lands in the San Gabriels. When he was hired in 1911 as the county's first trained forester (and later its fire warden), Stuart J. Flintham instigated an aggressive firefighting operation throughout the foothills; his strategy involved constructing lookout towers, creating an extensive network of firebreaks, and amassing tools and men to help suppress wildfire. He also promoted, in the aftermath of the big burns of the 1910s and early 1920s, reforestation and afforestation initiatives.

Convinced that if they could replace the Mediterranean-zone plants dominating the flammable landscape with pine and fir they might decrease the major fires that cyclically swept across this rugged terrain, and also slow hillside erosion, the county forester's office planted tens of thousands of seedlings.

After twenty years of backbreaking labor, and with little to show for it, the local agency abandoned the project. Flintham's successor, Spencer Turner, "was disillusioned with the high tree mortality," according to a county report, and recognized the "value of chaparral as a precious watershed cover that perhaps is fire dependent and best adapted to the site."

In 1930, three years after Turner and his colleagues paid tribute to the late Flintham's devoted service by planting in his memory a twenty-acre Coulter pine plantation in the Angeles National Forest, the new chief issued a restraining order: his foresters henceforth would "plant less, plant better."

The Forest Service has not quite learned LA County's hard-won lesson. Despite what federal foresters long have understood about the low fertility of local soils, the region's mercurial weather patterns, and steep canyon walls, they have repeatedly endeavored to reengineer the San Gabriels' ground cover.

Early in the twentieth century, they collaborated with county efforts to plant seedlings in this rough terrain, with predictable results: "In the 1920s, a million trees including exotic Canary Island pines were planted in the San Gabriel Mountains in a misguided effort to fix something that was not a problem—a predominance of native chaparral," notes Richard Halsey. "Most of those trees died because of drought."

Undaunted, as the smoke cleared from a 1960 blaze that roared through upper San Dimas Canyon, agency researchers decided again that chaparral had to go. As part of a revegetation project, scientists at the San Dimas Experimental Forest randomly selected eight watersheds to seed with annual grasses and eight with perennial grasses; four were left untouched as a control group. What they (re)discovered was that native plant material is a fierce competitor.

To restrain its competitive energy, the research team sprayed the grass-planted watersheds with herbicides, a strategy that comes with two ironies. The first is cultural: Rachel Carson's *Silent Spring* had just been published, a book that decried the poisoning of America's waterways and life systems in which the agency was complicit. The second is ecological: whatever the downstream consequences of the herbicidal spray, upslope the grasses' growth rate slowed over the project's lifetime, and despite the chemical assault they endured, indigenous plants took root and won out.

Back in the set of control-group watersheds, chaparral, manzanita, buckwheat, ceanothus, deervetch, and morning glory—which began sprouting within ten days of the fire—did even better. After four years these and other opportunistic plants had revegetated approximately 50 percent of the burned watersheds, a speed of recovery and density of cover that modern technology could not come close to replicating.

The researchers did not fully accept the evidence their studies revealed; instead, they insisted that under ideal conditions—ample rain, significant labor, and chemical applications—the "land managers would have been justified in trying to establish a grass crop." Still, they admitted, "this treatment should not be taken as a cure-all."

Why this institutional memory has not surfaced to check the Forest Service's current aspirations to reforest portions of the Angeles is an open question. More to the point, the agency's century-long inability to rearrange the San Gabriels' biota to its liking is a powerful rejoinder to those who so confidently believe that planting trees, indiscriminately and in large number, will help resolve some of the challenges that a climate-changed world is bringing. After all, when some of this planet's most accomplished land managers have had a hard time getting it right, it's difficult to believe that modern-day Johnny Appleseeds will do better.

If the tree planters persist, however, their success will depend on how they approach their self-appointed task. Only the humblest will have a chance, for at least they will recognize that they'll be mucking with complex ecosystems whose mysteries we have yet to comprehend.

What they will need most of all is the kind of knee-bending humility evoked in the final line of the poem earlier I promised not to quote: ". . . only God can make a tree."

Strawberry Fields Forever

Brunch was boisterous. Old friends from San Antonio were in town and we gathered around the dining room table in full view of our sun-drenched backyard, munching an array of spring-fresh, locally grown fruits and vegetables. The conversation was fast, funny, and convivial, but in a rare quiet moment one of our Texas guests asked what we had done to the strawberries—what made them so sweet: sugar? "Nothing added," my wife said, and smiled. "This is how they grow in Southern California."

Like the rest of the residents of the academic arcadia of Claremont, we have been spoiled by the flowering presence of a local strawberry patch; Vargas Farms has long managed the site, slotted on a rectangular set of six acres running parallel to the 210 freeway and framed to the west and north by Towne Avenue and Base Line Road.

I've loved walking by it in the early morning hours of winter, watching the crews build up the beds and lay down the irrigation system, labor overseen by bustling bands of killdeer birds that zigzagged across the fertile land. Their alarm call, a taut, nasal *kill-dee, kill-dee, kill-dee*, pierced even the rumble-whine of traffic beyond.

None of that energy, human or avian, was on display the other day. Weeds now choke the untended rows, the white pipes and sprinkler heads have vanished, and no killdeer raised their sharp voices. Come spring, every spring, we will have to hunt for a new vendor of that tender, succulent berry.

The farm fell victim to a postrecession land rush that almost in a blink of an eye converted a number of large empty lots in Claremont. Six developments, totaling nearly seven hundred new housing units, were announced in 2013, and by early 2015 most had been completed. One of these, slated to include more than ninety townhomes, was planned for the former strawberry field.

Such infill development, its rapid expansion notwithstanding, has its benefits. Among these upsides, as any New Urbanist will declare, is increased population density. With more people living within a smaller footprint the odds go up for a decrease in daily auto travel and a greater demand for mass transit. This may enhance ridership of local bus routes and the Metrolink, the regional suburban train network, one line of which runs from San Bernardino to the east, with a stop at Claremont's historic depot, before ending up in Union Station in downtown LA. Over the long term, there should also be a larger constituency demanding the eastward expansion of Metro Rail's Gold Line, light-rail that links Union Station with Pasadena, which over time is projected to swing through Claremont on its way east to Ontario airport.

Another set of related advantages is that those inhabiting these new developments will use fewer resources—most crucially, energy and water. Because they are choosing to live closer in, rejecting housing options available on the distant urban periphery that has radiated out from the Inland Empire's complex of freeways, the conversion of this particular truck farm may signal a market-driven slowing down of the decades-long assault on the eastern desert.

To entice those consumers alert to these possibilities and pressures, City Ventures, a regional developer, planned to add some attractive sustainability elements to its plans for the strawberry patch. As it has for its existing Southland projects, the company proposed planting drought-tolerant landscapes, installing solar arrays on the roofs, and building an "ocean-friendly" stormwater retention structure. These amenities and efficiencies, City Ventures asserted, added up to a win-win: "Less driving, clean air, close to everything you love and more time for the good things in life."

The car will not be erased from this smart-growth terrain: plans left plenty of room for Angelenos' four-wheeled love object, via lanes that were to snake through the project and the square footage that parking was to absorb.

The air will not be quite crystal-clear, either, given that this development hugs the heavily trafficked 210 freeway. The Claremont City Council earlier had rejected a proposal to construct much-needed affordable housing on this precise site on environmental-justice grounds: why should the less well-off only find shelter adjacent to a polluted highway's slipstream? (A sole representative reiterated this objection to the new project, which now lacks a meaningful number of affordable-housing units; did his colleagues in the majority feel that the middling class is somehow more immune to tailpipe emissions?)

Strangely enough, no one on the council strongly objected to another complication of the community's impending loss of open space, wherever located. As these properties were leveled, then platted, with roads scored into the ground and foundations poured and framing hammered in place, as these properties were built out and sold, their new residents' vehicles have surged onto the local street grid, jamming roadways and pounding roadbeds, a crowding that has had clear implications for traffic, tempers, and taxes.

These contemporary dilemmas are part and parcel of an older narrative about the physical restructuring of Los Angeles since World War II. After all, it was the internal-combustion engine that plowed under the region's one-time agricultural productivity. Its poisonous emissions were an equal opportunity killer: citrus groves, vineyards, and fruits and vegetables—to say nothing of the human pulmonary system—wilted before its fatal fumes, giving growers a negative incentive to decamp for clearer climes.

They were pushed out as well by city codes and county ordinances that prioritized residential development, much like the midcentury, auto-centric neighborhood where I now live; all such housing was accessed easily by the expanding number of freeways that reinforced the primacy of gas-guzzling vehicles.

In Claremont and the other foothill communities that line the southern face of the San Gabriel Mountains, that transition was quick and disorienting. During the early 1970s, while studying at Pitzer College, a member of the Claremont Consortium, my friends and I would ride bikes along Base Line Road past acre after acre of orange and lemon trees, through whose sweet fragrance we happily pedaled. Less than a decade later, those blossoming orchards were gone, bulldozed for cul-de-sac subdivisions.

Vestiges remain, smaller lots that an earlier generation of builders bypassed, deeming them too marginal, too unprofitable. Today, this acreage commands top dollar; one of these new, if cramped, sites abutting the 210 freeway is called Citrus Glen at Pitzer Ranch—an evocative name for a world we have lost.

Canyon Echoes

We hiked up San Dimas Canyon in search of the past.

It was impossible to miss some of its etchings, most obviously those cut into the ground by the now-vanished community that once fit within this narrow, steep-walled canyon formed by the west fork of the San Dimas River, a tributary of the San Gabriel.

Framing our route were the river-rock foundations of cabins that had housed upwards of ninety families on land leased from the Angeles National Forest. Vinca minor, an exotic vine with periwinkle-blue flowers, crawls over the gutted structures, cast-off kitchenware, and exposed nooks and crannies; climbing up the eastern and western slopes are sturdy clumps of cacti left to fend for themselves after these residences were gutted by the 2002 Williams Fire, a blaze that ultimately torched the entire watershed.

As for the road that had snaked along the San Dimas, it too had fallen victim to the conflagration: intense post-fire flooding and erosion has taken out most of its bed, and what remains is almost impassable; we had to clamber over alders, oaks, and pines that have dropped like pick-up sticks to block its meandering route.

A ghostly community: its silence shattered when a red-tailed hawk coasted overhead and let out a hoarse scream.

These communal artifacts, as haunting as the raptor's cry, were not the ones we were seeking. Instead our small party of three had set off from the Forest Service's San Dimas fire station hoping to relocate a memorial plaque erected in 1927 on an upstream hillside honoring Stuart J. Flintham.

The first professional forester and chief of what would become the Los Angeles County Fire Department, Flintham was a central figure in the establishment of the region's modern firefighting operations and the fostering of interagency cooperation between county and federal land managers. Earlier he had worked for the U.S. Forest Service, and it was therefore apt that my guides on this excursion were members of these same two agencies.

Better than apt: in Herman Garcia and J. Lopez, I was decidedly lucky. A Forest Service fire-engine captain, Herman has worked on the Angeles for most of his thirty-two-year career; along with J., a longtime forester for the LA County Fire Department, he made certain I didn't do damage to myself—always a live possibility. Along the way the two men shared their considerable knowledge about the canyon's complex weave of human and ecological history.

To recover these older stories had required a Google search. While hunting online for additional information about the New York native, a reference popped up for the Flintham Memorial Forest Plantation near San Dimas. I'd never heard of it and immediately sent an email to forester Lopez asking if he knew anything about the place; while he began asking around among his colleagues, I started roaming through the *Los Angeles Times*'s electronic archives for references to its establishment.

We struck pay dirt at the same time: I came upon a 1927 photograph of Flintham's young daughters, Dorothy and Eleanor, standing before a stone-studded memorial marker commemorating their late father's achievements. Meanwhile, J. had heard through the grapevine that in 2000 a Forest Service employee named Herman Garcia had guided one of Flintham's granddaughters to the site, seventy-three years after her mother and aunt had posed for the *Los Angeles Times* photographer.

Much had changed since that flashbulb had popped, and nothing illuminates this backstory better than the pine plantation itself.

It had been the brainchild of the Angeles Forest Protection Association, a volunteer support group for the national forest, which secured permission from U.S. Department of Agriculture Secretary William Marion Jardine to locate the memorial on a knoll (elevation: 2,180 feet) that rises above the canyon floor. As revealed in photographic evidence from the opening ceremony archived in the San Dimas Historical Society, the widely spaced, four-foot Coulter pines the association planted had a lot of room to grow, and in what proved to be prime conditions: the species, which can reach 80 feet in height, likes dry rocky soil (check); prefers a south-facing slope (check); and flourishes best at an elevation between 600 and 7,500 feet (check).

This physical setting came with biographical significance. Flintham had helped fight the 1919 San Dimas Fire, an inferno that opened up the hillside on which the posthumous plaque would be erected. This fire, along with others that summer, had exposed flaws in the region's fire-fighting capacities: "If there was ever a 'straw that broke the camel's back,'" observes fire historian David Boucher in *Ride the Devil Wind* (1991), "the fires of 1919 were it, as far as the organization of fire protection in Los Angeles County was concerned." In the smoky aftermath, county supervisors expanded Flintham's job title—the forester took over the responsibilities previously assigned to the fire warden and the fish and game warden—new work that allowed him to better coordinate local responses to wildfires in the San Gabriels.

Once planted on that stony grade, the Coulter pines grew. They continued to flourish even though a portion burned during a 1960 wildfire that swept across the upper San Dimas Canyon, blackening most of the Forest Service's adjacent San Dimas Experimental Forest. The plantation was largely intact forty years later when

Herman Garcia and Flintham's granddaughter came to pay their respects.

By then, Herman estimated, many of the pines measured thirty inches in diameter, a towering presence on the hillside; so dense was the twenty-acre forest that the visitors had to circle around the entire expanse before they found the memorial, set on its southeastern corner.

It's there still.

Nothing else remains. That's because two years later the Williams Fire incinerated the plantation during its week-long run through 38,000 acres of chaparral and manzanita, alder, pine, and oak. Herman was on the frontlines throughout the inferno, battling its flames from Tanbark Flats high above the canyon near Glendora Mountain Road down to the cluster of cabins whose gutted foundations we would hike past a decade later.

He recalled the tearful plea of one resident, as she evacuated before the wall of flames and embers swept in, that he please, please save her house. The *Los Angeles Daily News* recounted his creative heroics: "He held a fire at bay on one roof with water from a backpack. After the pack was empty, Garcia hunted inside the cabin for water. A pot of chicken broth was on the stove. He used that and then scooped water from the toilet. Though that cabin was saved, most others—more than 70, at last count—are rubble."

Out of the wreckage, up from that scorched environs, has come new life. That's what J. helped me appreciate.

His encyclopedic knowledge of fire-zone ecology—of the changes that big burns can bring to a landscape, to its plants, animals, and hydrology—opened up a larger discussion about the kinds of adaptations and regenerative strategies that can turn gray ash into green shoots. Alders have sprouted in the riparian habitat; chaparral, sagebrush, and ceanothus are reclaiming slopes and drainage features; yerba santa and raspberries have occupied once-disturbed areas; everywhere butterflies flit and lizards scoot.

But the hardiest reclamation agent is the scrub oak. That's the clothes-snagging lesson I was about to learn when, after hiking for a couple of miles along the gurgling river, Herman spotted a tall, unburned Coulter pine hugging the western bank of the San Dimas. It sparked a memory: somewhere around this spot, he and Stuart Flintham's granddaughter had started climbing.

They at least had the plantation to guide them uphill; we had no such pointers.

With nary a pause, Herman headed up, red-bladed brushcutter in hand, opening the way as we switchbacked along the steep grade. The loose soil and brittle rock so characteristic of the San Gabriels added to the difficulty of our movement (as did my klutziness—J. hauled me out of any number of thorny run-ins with that tough flora). After thirty minutes or so, Herman shouted that he had found what we had been seeking: his GPS-like memory led him to clear a trail to within two feet of the memorial.

Absent a few of its rivets that had popped out when the Williams inferno turned the air into a furnace, the brass plaque appeared unscathed. The monument in which it is embedded could not have been more prominently placed. Scanning the horizon to the south, we could see straight down the canyon into the San Gabriel Valley; Mount Baldy, its flanks glistening with snow, anchored the north and east; and to the west arose a brush-choked ridge separating the San Dimas and Big Dalton watersheds.

What remained of the former pine plantation was difficult to discern; decaying trunks lay hidden beneath impenetrable growth of scrub oak. One such prickly copse revealed a surprising juxtaposition: next to a bleached stump grew a five-foot Coulter pine, a blue-green wedge pushing up into the cloudless sky.

This affirmation of renewal came with a subtle reminder of the indelible bonds between then and now. Heading back downhill, I skidded into a gnarled oak, held fast, and pressed my nose into its charred bark: a faint, acrid whiff of the past.

Creek Bed

I heard the water splashing long before I saw its fall. The sound—a clear, thin cascade—drew me east toward the dawn as I moved up the gravel-rough horse trail paralleling Thompson Creek diversion channel in northern Claremont. Streaming west in the concrete bed was a slow flow from the previous day's rain: I knew more about how these waters would get to the Pacific than I did about their source.

The deep ditch drops away from Thompson Creek dam, one of a number of flood-control structures built in the aftermath of the devastating 1938 flood that crashed through Claremont and much of the Pomona Valley and wreaked havoc through the Southland. The channel cuts along the base of the foothills before turning south into the city of Pomona, where it merges with other ditches and culverts, an infrastructure that swings past Ganesha Park and Cal Poly–Pomona and then slides by nondescript warehouses and industrial parks before slipping between low-lying hills in Pomona's southwestern quadrant. As it pushes past La Puente, City of Industry, and Avocado Heights, this long-running channel finally converges with the San Gabriel River hard by the 60 and 605 freeway interchange, a multilayered intersection of the riparian and vehicular.

From that confluence, it is a relatively straight shot to the sea. But not so the movement of water into this artery-like construction, a branch of which I hoped to trace that early weekend morning. The splish-splashing I heard signaled I was close to Sycamore Canyon and the unnamed creek that over the millennia has given shape to the rough floor through which it trickles and the manzanita-choked walls that rise above.

Crossing the short bridge that leads over the Thompson Creek ditch and into the canyon's mouth, I was struck that there is nothing particularly unusual about the 144-acre site as a landform; it is one of hundreds of wedge-shaped ravines that give contour to the San Gabriel foothills.

As best anyone knows, nothing of great significance has happened at this spot, either.

For the Tongva, who hunted and gathered across the broad expanse from present-day San Bernardino to the Santa Monica highlands, it was among many coastal sage scrub ecosystems whose resources nurtured their daily life. Here, as elsewhere, they found meat and fish, fur, berries, nuts, and seeds, bark from sycamores and manzanita, leaves from sage and buckwheat.

The communities sustained by this plenty began to diminish with the arrival of the Spanish missions, and the diseases and technologies they unpacked in the inland valleys of the Los Angeles basin. As the indigenous people wilted before imported pathogens and were conscripted as labor for new forms of sedentary agriculture, Spanish ranching operations began to mow down the hillside and canyonland habitats through the grazing of sheep, goats, and cattle. It is doubtful whether they or their colonizing replacements, the Euro-Americans who flooded into gold-rush California in the mid-nineteenth century, paid any special attention to this narrow gap in the foothills.

Sycamore Canyon would have remained undistinguished and indistinguishable had its upper folds not been bulldozed and flattened for the construction of a mid-twentieth-century upscale development dubbed Claraboya. To domesticate the ridgelines and outcroppings that surround its high-priced homes, the new residents started planting nonnative trees, shrubs, and grasses, all heavily irrigated. The outflow of fertilizer-laden water nourished the spread of invasives down the slopes and not incidentally tainted the canyon's creek. The increased density of woody vegetation turned the crests of these once-golden hills emerald, a chromatic shift that spelled trouble in fall 2003.

Late that October, a firestorm erupted across Southern California, fueled by strong winds and a desiccated landscape that had not burned in decades. One of the massive conflagrations, the Old–Grand Prix–Padua Fire, torched upwards of 170,000 acres along the southern flank of the San Bernardino and San Gabriel Mountains, killed six people, destroyed more than 1,000 homes, and cost over $50 million to suppress.

Among the many neighborhoods that were evacuated in advance of the rapidly moving fire was Claraboya. The precautionary move was a good thing: more than a dozen houses there were incinerated as the inferno swept from crown to crown, and crackled through the thick underbrush. Sycamore Canyon became a swirling cauldron, shooting flames up a ladder of vegetation to engulf residences above.

When the fire was contained in early November, the canyon was a smoldering ruin. Its slopes were charred, and along the creek, toppled in a maze, were the blackened trunks of eucalyptus, oak, and sycamore. On the same day that Claraboya residents were allowed to drive up the aptly named Mountain Avenue to inspect the damage, city officials issued an advisory: "Anyone wanting to access Thompson Creek Trail should do so only with great caution as there is damage to much of the area surrounding the trail." The Padua Fire had been so destructive that Sycamore Canyon was sealed off for the next ten years.

It was finally reopened in mid-2013 after a multiyear reclamation project. Cleanup had begun almost immediately after the fire had been subdued. In the mid-2000s, the forestry division of the Los Angeles County Fire Department reintroduced grazing to the area, managing a herd of goats to reduce vegetation fire hazards on unburned slopes below Claraboya. In collaboration with the City of Claremont and the Los Angeles Conservation Corps, its Camp 19 hand crews then moved in to clear away debris, particularly the stuff that had crashed into the creek, and reestablish a single-track trail that snakes into the canyon, and another running uphill that ultimately connects to the 1,620-acre Claremont Hills Wilderness Park that lies to the north.

The most sensitive part of the agency's work, which hewed to the city's commitment to restoring the area's native ecosystem, was to remove thirty-five dead or dying eucalyptus that originally had been planted or seeded in the rocky soil. Their removal for reasons of public safety was followed by a phased logging of another one hundred eucalyptus that had survived the 2003 fire. This two-stage harvest was essential, consultants from BonTerra informed the city, for "eucalyptus trees release chemicals into the surrounding soil that inhibit the establishment of understory plants," a biological defense mechanism that would undermine the "regeneration of the park." Removing these trees would give Sycamore Canyon a better chance of recovering its indigenous habitat.

That restoration project has required additional human intervention, a hand everywhere evident as I hiked into the canyon. Controlling winter rain-generated debris flows that can carom down scorched and eroded slopes required the building of a substantial steel-and-timber barrier, embedded in concrete blocks, that now spans the lower creek to protect the flood channel into which it flows. Upstream, earthen check-dams have been built to further arrest churning waters.

The planting of 360 oak and sycamore seedlings within the riparian zone is noteworthy too, for the goal has been to replicate the canyon's historic canopy and root structure, bringing much-needed shade to summer-heated soils and stabilizing banks and slopes. Landscape architect Mark von Wodtke, cofounder of the Claremont Environmental Design Group and a contributing partner to the restoration project, enthused to the *Claremont Courier*: "We have been able to demonstrate, here in this canyon, how we are able to regenerate nature and the natural environment."

This regenerative aspiration—like the even more ambitious project that the National Forest Foundation, the U.S. Forest Service, and a host of partners are conducting in the Big Tujunga watershed, which was badly burned in the 2009 Station Fire—marks a significant turning point in our understanding of what water means in, to, and for Southern California.

So it occurred to me when, after tramping about a mile along the canyon floor, I retraced my steps, following the creek's low-pitched gurgle to where it pooled in a depression before draining into a pipe that sluiced it into the Thompson Creek flood-control channel—and from which that morning it spilled so musically.

The difference between the restored creek bed and the concrete ditch is not simply that one is organic and the other engineered, though that's true enough. It is a little more complicated to acknowledge that these two systems are intertwined, or hybridized, and that they also reflect differing conceptions of our role in managing water in the semi-arid Southland.

The Thompson Creek channel has had but one purpose: to capture any and all runoff and flush it to the ocean as fast as possible. Its developers did not worry about how ecologically sound the upper reaches of its watershed was. What mattered was moving the wet stuff from the moment it hits the ground to the split second before the San Gabriel River rushes into the Pacific at Seal Beach. Theirs was a technocratic impulse and imperative.

The restoration of Sycamore Canyon is every bit as managerial in its motivation and orientation. Foresters, ecologists, landscape designers, and planners—experts all—have rearranged hillside and creek bed, selected which tree species should be logged and which should be cultivated, and used goats, chainsaws, shovels, hammers, and nails to build a model terrain.

The difference between these visions lies not in tools but in intent. Shaped by the history of damaging floods, mid-twentieth-century engineers defined moving water as a danger or a waste; efforts to control the former or get rid of the latter were built into the complex web of dams, culverts, ditches, and channels that give shape to modern Los Angeles.

Yet for all its effectiveness, this rigid plumbing system also robs the land of its health; by diverting water away from local aquifers, by straitjacketing once free-flowing rivers, it disables these natural systems and the ecological communities that depended on them.

Hurt too is the public's health, a claim that is tied to an all-encompassing ecological ethic planted with each seedling on this small patch of ground inside the Thompson Creek watershed. "We abuse land because we regard it as a commodity belonging to us," Aldo Leopold argues in *A Sand County Almanac.* "When we see land as a community to which we belong, we may begin to use it with love and respect." Essential to that feeling of respect is accepting that our use "is right when it tends to preserve the integrity, stability, and beauty of the biotic community. It is wrong when it tends otherwise."

In Sycamore Canyon, Claremont has been trying to get it right.

Wet Dreams

William Mulholland, who supervised the planning and construction of the Los Angeles Aqueduct, the flow of which would power the city's politics, nurture its industrialization, and transform its semi-arid landscape, was not a garrulous man.

"This rude platform is an altar," Mulholland told a jubilant crowd of 30,000 gathered in the foothills of the San Gabriel Mountains to celebrate the aqueduct's dedication on November 5, 1913, "and on it we are here consecrating this water supply and dedicating the Aqueduct to you and your children and your children's children—for all time." Although this sentence sounded like the start of a lengthy paean to that present day's shimmering future, it marked the beginning and end of his speech: "That's all," he said, and then sat down to thunderous applause.

At least those were the words he uttered for the mass of men, women, and children who had traveled by automobile, train, and horse and buggy to get their first look at and taste of Sierra snowmelt channeled from the Owens River Valley more than 230 miles to the north of the City of Angels. As the throng surged toward the infrastructure to cheer the first gallons cascading down a nearby hill, Mulholland turned to Mayor J. J. Rose and reportedly urged: "There it is, Mr. Mayor. Take it."

Los Angeles took it, and then some. Since 1913, it has imported millions of acre-feet of water via this system, and its extension in the 1930s farther north to tap Mono Lake and its tributaries. A decade earlier, the city funded another lengthy pipeline to the east to siphon water out of the Colorado River. And in 1919 the idea was first floated to build a massive state water project that would divert water out of the Sacramento River delta and send it through the Central Valley, up and over the Tehachapi Mountains, and into Southern California, a hotly debated concept that would take fifty years to bring to fruition.

To commemorate and critique the aqueduct's centennial, a colleague and I collaborated on an exhibition of photographs and documents that focused particularly on the first act of this long-running drama. Our choice of images to introduce the subject, and the long-standing controversy that has surrounded it, was as deliberate as it was telling, a conscious framing.

The first was a bird's-eye view of pueblo Los Angeles in the 1850s—spare, dry, and compact—juxtaposed to another from the 1920s that by implication introduced the postaqueduct terrain, a verdant and sprawling landscape of orange groves and suburban subdivisions, an irrigated Eden where "water is neither scarce nor dear." There were (and remain) unstated costs in the wiping out of native ecosystems and biological diversity in the Owens River Valley and in Southern California, some of which are captured in the swirling mists of imported water sprayed on manicured lawns, but those benefiting from these imported waters rarely stopped to think about such consequences.

Among those happy to ignore the deficits that the LA Aqueduct might impose were those urban boosters most loudly touting its many incontrovertible benefits. Power brokers such as Mulholland, Fred Eaton, and J. B. Lippincott, along with a host of politicos, entrepreneurs, and industrialists, operated according to a simple calculation: water equaled growth. And growth was good, as defined by such indicators as increases in population, economic activity, and living standards. That would seem an easy sell, yet to secure the funding necessary to build the massive conduit required an extensive "campaign to make the aqueduct popular." To sway voters, aqueduct advocates unleashed a sophisticated media blitz, rallied local chambers of commerce, and to all promoted the tantalizing prospects of unbridled wealth and unlimited opportunity that the aqueduct would generate.

Persuasive, too, were the blueprints, photographs, topographical maps, and other illustrative evidence of the project's technological ambitions; it created an engineered landscape that moved vast quantities of water and kilowatts of electricity across a rugged terrain, demonstrating anew the human capacity to subordinate nature to our very material ends.

Surely it is not by happenstance, too, that at the same time Los Angeles was falling in love with auto-mobility and constructing a new street grid to speed its residents' movement across the land, it was also constructing a complex system of pipes, dams, tunnels, and channels to rush water into the community's many new orchards, factories, and parks, its sinks, bathtubs, and greenswards.

However giddy were the aqueduct's prospects and realities, its development was not contest free. Many residents of the Owens River Valley fought long and hard against the transfer of their water resources by means peaceful and violent. Through open appeals to the state and nation, they sought redress for what they knew to be a "Valley of Broken Hearts," pleas that fell on deaf ears in Sacramento and Washington, DC.

Sharing Owens Valley activists' critique of LA's water grab were folks living to the city's immediate east. They were convinced that local watersheds can and should be managed locally and sustainably. Making clever use of Southern California's geology, particularly the alluvial washes that swept out of the canyons of the San Gabriel Mountains, organizations such as the Pomona Valley Protective Association maintained these geological features as open space. Winter rains and runoff would then filter into this gravelly soil, replenishing the aquifers buried below; these basins "resembled very much the ordinary restaurant dinner plate with separate receptacles for different foods," one contemporary observed, and he believed they offered the region its best hope for survival.

Preferring human-built structures to natural cisterns, a choice in concert with their narrative of domination and control, Los Angeles's legion of promoters instead ratcheted up their commitment to concrete action. Certain that the aqueduct needed an additional reservoir to protect against the region's episodic droughts and ongoing sabotage of the aqueduct in the Owens Valley, in the early 1920s Mulholland, a self-taught engineer, helped design the St. Francis Dam in the San Francisquito Canyon in the Santa Clara River watershed north of the city.

Completed in 1926, it impounded an estimated 38,000 acre-feet of water. Within hours of Mulholland's certifying its structural integrity on March 12, 1928, the dam collapsed—tragically, in the middle of the night; it unleashed a killer surge of water that crashed down the narrow canyon before blasting into the Santa Clara River.

"It seems probable that the flood peak immediately below the dam exceeded half a million second-feet," a subsequent engineering report intoned, "and this, together with its occurrence in the darkness, and the suddenness and violence of the wave, was such that very few of the persons in the constricted valley below the dam escaped with their lives." More than six hundred people perished that evening; many of their bodies were never found.

Although this horrific disaster destroyed Mulholland's reputation, it did not damage the citizenry's belief in his ambitious effort to import ever-larger amounts of water to slake the city's deepening thirst. Voters easily passed bond issues in support of the Colorado Aqueduct and the Mono Lake project, setting the stage for additional investments in the second half of the twentieth century, a legacy that has proved pivotal to the making of what is now the nation's second largest city.

That end, the aqueduct's original proponents would have asserted, justified their heavy-handed means.

Thinking Like a Watershed

What makes local, local? We know what "county" or "state" or "nation" is, by the precise boundaries that separate these entities from one another; "international" is just as bounded. But "local" lacks any such geographical demarcation. It is not a city or town (though it could be); it is more a cultural assumption about a place, an emotional tie, a perspective—boundless.

Yet determining where "local" is, and what it means, is critical to understanding its significance in contemporary American environmental discourse. This is a vital exercise in large part because the term has become a mantra of sorts, regularly chanted at formal conferences and informal gatherings whose subject is the future of the human presence on earth. It has become the locus of activism, the locale of hope.

Credit climate change, that most global of forces, with offering us an opportunity to rebuild our communities and reconstruct our democracy, from the ground up.

But which ground is the preferred one? How are we to define what is local and thus identify the sustaining origin of a steadier life on what activist Bill McKibben calls a tough new planet? The answer, for those of us living in the American West, may lie not in new ideas of the future but in an older concept dating from the mid-nineteenth century.

That's when John Wesley Powell, second head of the U.S. Geological Survey (now U.S. Geological Service, or USGS), led the now-legendary expedition down the Colorado River, rafting its rapids over the spring and summer of 1869. His voyage and subsequent explorations of the dry regions of the interior West led Powell to argue that a new political structure was necessary if Americans intended to live in terrain of such scant precipitation. As he floated past the rough and rocky landforms, which we can more easily envision while flying across the continent, Powell identified water's definitive power. "In a group of mountains a small river has its source," he noted in his landmark *Report on the Lands in the Arid Region of the United States* (1876). "A dozen or a score of creeks unite to form the trunk. The creeks higher up divide into brooks. All these streams combined form the drainage system of the hydrographic basin, a unit of country well defined in nature, for it is bounded above and on each side by heights of land that rise as crests to part the waters. Thus hydraulic basin is segregated from hydraulic basin by nature herself, and the landmarks are practically perpetual."

This physical structure had decided political implications, Powell believed: the only settlement pattern that made sense in the West was one framed inside the region's many watersheds. Land-ownership patterns, and political and social systems, should be slotted within their boundaries.

Because each such district would become "a commonwealth by itself," Powell declared, out of this would emerge "a body of interdependent and unified interests and values, all collected in one hydraulic basin, and all segregated by well-defined boundary lines from the rest of the world." United by "common interests, common rights, and common duties," the residents "would work together for common purposes." Should the "entire arid region be organized into natural hydrographic districts," its environmental constraints would compel the creation of a more direct democracy, a more virtuous public space.

No one listened to Powell. But that's not the point. More to the point is that he was correct in his supposition that watershed commonwealths—as opposed to the artificial imposition of state borders, county lines, and city limits—would have been a saner way to delineate communal life in this land of little rain. His ideal is even more relevant now, given the intense pressures bearing down on the American West, portions of which have been suffering from historic droughts since 2010; this dryness, as climate models reveal, will define much of the twenty-first century, too.

This will have a significant impact on the U.S. West, which for the last century has been building water-distribution systems that have cost billions of dollars to construct and maintain, systems that consume massive amounts of energy to move water across valley and desert, and up and down mountains. (California's State Water Project, for instance, is the largest consumer of energy in the state: every acre-foot of water lifted over the Tehachapi Mountains and distributed across Southern California burns upwards of 3,000 kilowatt-hours of electricity.) This complex infrastructure, developed for interbasin transfers of white gold, may no longer function as it once did. The key dilemma is whether those basins—and more precisely the high country that rings them, from the Rockies and Wasatch to the Sierra—will continue to receive the levels of precipitation that once made them skiers' heavens and icy reservoirs for the communities below.

The latest data from the Intergovernmental Panel on Climate Change (IPCC) suggest otherwise, and as the already arid portions of the West dry up, the region's megacities like Los Angeles will be in considerable trouble (and places like El Paso and Albuquerque already are). No wonder, then, that the USGS (Powell's old outfit) has been evaluating local groundwater supplies in Southern California, seeking ways to protect these once-ignored resources. Its efforts are a reminder that the aquifers underlying central and western sections of the city once offered plenteous amounts of water (and today still supply 30–40 percent of the daily take).

Developing strategies for replenishing these underground resources, like Friends of the LA River's three-decade-long effort to get us to imagine the Los Angeles River as a river, are parts of a larger transformation. Where once fiefdoms dominated the region's water politics, where exclusive preserves deliberately ignored hydraulic realities, these artificial barriers appear to be breaking down. Practitioners and activists are now working across these demarcations, cooperating with one-time competitors, adopting each other's best practices. Unfazed by the lack of clear state policy prescriptions or federal mandates, they are collaborating upstream and down, between basins, and across state borders.

This collaboration has important implications, for seeing ourselves as inhabitants of watersheds and river basins is an essential step toward recognizing that these topographical features are the building blocks—metaphorical and real—of life on this climate-changed earth. And because they are also our home ground, there is nothing more local.

Water Fights

Call it Oregon Envy. I first heard of this syndrome from contractors and landscapers who laughingly described its central symptoms: emerald lawns in a brown terrain; two hundred inches a year of irrigated rain in a place that receives less than fifteen inches naturally; a hunger to turn arid Southern California into the lush Pacific Northwest.

There is no landscape more lush than Claremont, the quaint college town on the eastern edge of Los Angeles County that likes to call itself the City of Trees and PhDs. The community nurtures a dense canopy, framed around its street trees; every road has a dedicated species— camphor or elm, ginkgo, oak, or crape myrtle, sycamore or liquidambar—and the city will give you the relevant sapling should your front yard be so lacking. This arboreal fetish would be impossible to maintain without a reliable, plentiful, and cheap supply of water.

That gush has only been available for the past seventy years or so. Aerial photographs of the Pomona Valley dating back to the late 1920s reveal just how few trees, orange groves notwithstanding, dotted the landscape; its relative starkness reflected its aridity. That generation lived within their watershed and its means.

Not so now. The present-day thick settlement and thicket of greenery are a direct result of the larger region's successful efforts to tap ever-more-distant sources of water—first the Owens Valley and the eastern slope of the Sierra via the Los Angeles Aqueduct; then the Colorado River Aqueduct; and ultimately the State Water Project, drawing snowmelt from the northern Sierra. Since the mid-twentieth century, Claremont, like the Southland in general, has benefited enormously from the politics of water expropriation, and the massive investment in infrastructure that was its result. We paid good money to take other people's water so that our grass would be green, our pools full, and our shade luxuriously abundant.

Little wonder that when in fall 2011 the local purveyor, Golden State Water Company (GSWC)—a subsidiary of American States Water Company, a publicly traded company—announced that it was seeking permission to jack up its rates by 24.54 percent, many in the town went ballistic. A loosely organized group, complete with its own Facebook page (Claremonters Against Outrageous Water Rates), swiftly emerged.

Its members' outrage was understandable: amid a then still-biting recession, with unacceptably high unemployment levels, and a foreboding sense that it was getting harder and harder to make ends meet, especially for the poorest and those on fixed incomes, this was hardly the opportune time to inform customers that they would have to fork over more cash to pay for such an essential resource as water. In response, this set of aggrieved citizens pushed back, one mark of which was their sound-bite lawn sign: Stop the Golden State Water Rip-Off!

For its part, GSWC believed it was not bilking its monopolized clientele, but rather investing in the future: the increased rates it sought were targeted toward rebuilding what it described as its aging water infrastructure, an argument it has made across its service area, from Barstow in the Mojave Desert to Ojai, south and east of Santa Barbara.

In a more economically robust past, much of the funding for such necessary replacement and updating came from federal and/or state budgets. Those monies had evaporated with the Republican-led attack on earmarking of the congressional budget; earmarking had once been a crucial spigot that representatives had used to direct money to vital water projects in their districts. Another source under repeated assault from Tea Party budget-slashers has been the Environmental Protection Agency's Clean Water and Drinking Water State Revolving Funds, which once upon a time offered billions to state-priority projects to enhance public health and environmental cleanup. The evisceration of the California state budget also dried up another pool of capital investment.

Who was left to foot the very large bill? The rate-payers.

They are "paying for the power, the pump, to treat and move that water from the ground or from the reservoir," argued Susan Longville, director of the Water Resources Institute at nearby CSU–San Bernardino. And so they are also "paying for those carrying costs and the infrastructure that delivers it, and the water agencies just find themselves in the place where the rate the consumer is going to pay is the only place to turn."

That said, ratepayers always have paid these costs, albeit indirectly through a variety of taxing formulas at the state and federal levels. These mechanisms have masked our multiple contributions and decreased our individual share of these costs, spreading the burden across the region, state, and nation. Now the hurt has been magnified because it is directly borne by a precise population utilizing a particular water company, and in Claremont's case one whose shares are daily traded on the NY Stock Exchange. The monthly bill had morphed into a tax receipt, reflecting the very real cost of water in real time.

This situation will not change for those in Claremont (or their peers throughout the Inland Empire, who also have been hit with spiking water costs), even should they succeed in purchasing Golden State's local operations. On the contrary: if the city of 35,000 residents absorbs this responsibility—and in November 2014, after a frenzied campaign, local voters overwhelmingly supported Measure W, which authorized the city council to issue water revenue bonds up to $135 million to pay for the acquisition of the Claremont Water System from Golden State—it will not decrease water rates. Claremont will have to hire professionals to run and technicians to maintain its water-delivery systems; it will need to underwrite all expenses associated with evaluating and upgrading relevant pipes, pumps, and meters. There may be no savings to pass along to consumers; local control will be expensive.

Yet money is not everything. Local control will make Claremont, and communities like it, more nimble, more effective in responding to climate-distorted weather patterns. Although the region is currently predicted to receive about the same amount of precipitation over the rest of the century, whether it will be able to take advantage of that rainfall—and infiltrate it into local aquifers—is debatable; or at least it is under the current water regime, which depends on the importation of water from either the State Water System (which moves it south from the western slope of the Sierra) or from the Colorado River (and thus from Rocky Mountain snowmelt). Because the cost of this imported water is already rising, and is anticipated to increase across the foreseeable future, weaning ourselves off this flow makes good sense.

In this context, for example, community ownership, because it is not beholden to shareholders and not required to make a profit, is more able to invest in and incentivize the adoption of conservation measures that will ratchet down water use. Start with the water bill itself. One innovation that a Claremont-owned water system could adopt is that which the San Antonio, Texas, water system has long utilized: it provides each customer with data that compares their monthly water consumption with that of their immediate neighbors. If you want to keep up with the Joneses, you'll need to fix that leaky faucet or take shorter showers (and preferably both).

The city will also be much more willing than a for-profit entity to increase incentives that reimburse residential and commercial customers switching to low-flow toilets, showerheads, and drip-irrigation systems, as well as those who rip out water-sucking landscaping and replace it with drought-loving plant material; such practices are common throughout the Southwest, notably in Las Vegas. Finally, the city, unlike the corporation, will more quickly see the considerable advantage of launching a robust educational campaign through the schools and other social institutions about the pressing need for additional conservation measures, a sign of its commitment to building a water-wise community.

Put it another way: everyone in this region needs to know exactly how much it costs every time we wash the dishes, hose down a driveway, and soak the lawn. Acting on this vital information is the only way we will cut our consumption and reduce our costs. It is also the only way that we will wise up to the enviable, if dry, fact that Claremont is located in Southern California, not western Oregon.

Golden Shore

Whale Watching

Richard Henry Dana had a soft spot for Dana Point. Not because it was named for him—that honor came posthumously.

Rather, it was the small cove's isolation and solitude, its pounding waves, and massive rock formations, sheer and jagged, that struck him most: "There was a grandeur in everything around," he wrote in *Two Years before the Mast* (1841), a charming travelogue detailing his time aboard the *Pilgrim*; he was a regular Jack Tar on a Boston merchant ship that cruised along Alta California in the mid-1830s exchanging cattle hides for New England manufactured goods.

The stark setting "gave a solemnity to the scene, a silence and solitariness which affected every part!" he enthused. "Not a human being but ourselves for miles, and no sound heard but the pulsations of the great Pacific! And the great steep hill rising like a wall, and cutting us off from all the world, but the 'world of waters'!" The nineteen-year-old sailor was smitten; Bahia Capistrano, as it was then known, and San Juan Bay, which stretched from its rough shore, "is the only romantic spot on the coast."

Dana wouldn't recognize the place today, I thought while standing on the deck of the *Manute'a*, a sleek fifty-foot catamaran. We had come aboard to do a bit of whale watching on a bright and clear day in early January, drawn to Dana Point by reports of a spectacular run of gray whales along the Orange County coast.

No longer is the harbor quiet and sublime: its formidable cliffs remain, but they are now crowned with McMansions and adorned with thick green landscaping that muffles the spare, hard surfaces that had entranced Dana.

Once open to the sea—"it tumbled in," a thrilled Dana wrote, "roaring and spouting, among the crevices of the great rocks. What a sight, thought I, must this be in a southeaster!"—Dana Point is now framed behind a massive set of breakwaters. These rocky formations offer flatwater for innumerable paddleboarders and also shelter marinas jammed with the pleasure craft of the modern mariner—sloops and yawls, high-powered speedboats, cabin cruisers, and tour boats. Such as the *Manute'a*, whose winter business is structured around the southern migration of the California gray whale as they head to their historic feeding grounds in the bathtub-warm lagoons in the Gulf of California.

Although the news of increased sightings had brought us to Dana Point, we kept our hopes in check: previous outings from Long Beach and Newport Beach harbors had been disappointing. Sure, we had seen a whale or two, and pods of rollicking dolphins, but nothing we witnessed on those trips prepared us for what we would encounter on this one.

Fifteen minutes out of Dana Point, the show began, and it did so with a bit of misidentification: the captain shouted that he had spotted a large pod of dolphins off the port bow, only to discover as we slid closer that what he thought had been a roiling group of bottlenose turned out to be twenty or more sea lions, cavorting. Their playful antics proved a quiet interlude.

Ahead, maybe another mile south, the air and sea were in frantic turmoil. Thousands of pelagic birds—gulls, murres, pelicans, and terns—crisscrossed the skies, rising up and then dive-bombing the dark waters. Below, countless dolphins churned unseen, pushing schools of fish to the surface. This symbiotic feeding frenzy between mammal and avian, a so-called bait-ball, was as riveting as it was frustrating. Trying to identify the birds was impossible: their movements were so frenetic, their attacks so swift. This intense, noisy ballet of life and death, juxtaposed to the otherwise calm, flat seas, was such that had we circled north and returned to Dana Point I would have been happy.

But not as happy as I was when the captain urged us to tear our eyes away from that surging struggle for survival and scan the horizon: I was half hoping he would bellow "Thar she blows," but his more prosaic "I've spotted a pod of gray whales ahead" did the trick.

These magnificent creatures, who summer in the frigid waters of the far northern Pacific and then cruise south to mate, feed, and rear their young, grow to forty-five feet and weigh in at thirty to forty tons. Their annual transit along the long stretch of the Pacific Coast, during which they rack up 10,000 to 14,000 miles a year, has occurred for millennia. For just as long they have figured centrally in the oral traditions and foodways of the Alaskan native peoples; their harpoons, water craft, and hunting skills made these migrating mammals a key component in their diet.

Strikingly, the gray whale figures less crucially in the culture of the Chumash, a puzzling lacuna given that they too were deft mariners, regularly plying the turbulent waters between the Southern California coast and the Channel Islands. "The Chumash did not actively hunt whales," observes my colleague Jennifer Perry, an archaeologist who specializes in these ancient peoples' lives and livelihoods, "mostly because their boats are designed more for cargo capacity than speed, quite in contrast to the Inuit kayak. However, they and the Tongva regularly capitalized on stranded or beached whales, not just for food, but for building materials and tools. Whale bones were used to construct the frameworks for houses, as evidenced at sites on San Clemente Island."

A different kind of opportunism marked the industrialization of whaling in the early nineteenth century. Utilizing whale oil for illumination, bones for corsets, and a host of other material purposes, European and American investors sent hundreds of ships into the Pacific to kill, strip, and render these creatures into hulking carcasses, which they then dumped overboard—a foul wake.

Like most energy-resource booms, this one also crashed: so intense was the slaughter that whale populations collapsed, leading to a spike in the hunting costs that outran the return on investment by the early 1860s. It never recovered: the whaling fleet was pressed into service during the Civil War, and shortly after the end of hostilities, coal and petroleum became cheaper, more reliable sources of fuel and light.

Yet despite its brief, violent run, whaling launched a cultural type, a young man of means who sought himself and his fortune by heading out to sea. Among them were Herman Melville and Richard Henry Dana, who mined their youthful experiences on the bounding main for their novels (Melville's *Typee*, *Omoo*, and *Moby-Dick*) and memoirs (Dana's *Two Years before the Mast* and *Twenty-Four Years After*), a trafficking in literary commerce that turned the Pacific and the West Coast into an American Eden.

Dana made this case through the ubiquitous and gentle presence of gray whales in his narrative: "This being the spring season, San Pedro, as well as all the other open ports upon the coast, was filled with whales that had come in to make their annual visit upon soundings. For the first few days that we were here and at Santa Barbara, we watched them with great interest—calling out 'there she blows!' every time we saw the spout of one breaking the surface of the water; but they soon became so common that we took little notice of them."

Out west floated a Peaceable Kingdom.

No whaler would have been so benign, which makes Dana's initial excitement akin to the thrill that surged through those aboard the *Manute'a* when we neared the slow-moving pod of gray whales, a couple of miles off Laguna Beach.

As they blew and sounded, their white-blotched flukes on full display; as their dolphin escorts glided alongside us, knifing through the sun-flecked water with little visible effort; as gulls and pelicans and terns wheeled and dipped across cloudless skies, we drifted south, lost in time.

Our reverie was broken when a gray whale breached, thrusting its body up into the air before crashing back into the roughened waters. Rising behind it were the twin concrete domes of the San Onofre nuclear power plant, an odd tableau that sparked this thought: in that instant, my fellow passengers and I caught an illuminating glimpse of the history of energy use in the United States, from whale oil to atomic power.

We could see as well the dilemmas different generations confronted in their reliance on what each presumed was cheap energy, and the hidden costs they contained. San Onofre is now shut down, due to the expense associated with retrofitting the aging plant, bringing closure to those who long protested its dangers. Continued vigilance on behalf of the gray whales may bring similar relief: stringent regulations would help regenerate the whale population, a salubrious outcome, for although they currently number an estimated 22,000, that is less than half as many as were alive when the first whalers sailed into the Pacific.

Should they once again frolic and feed in the harbors and bays of the West Coast, a future writer may be able to observe as did C. H. Townsend in late 1885: "At the San Simeon station . . . I could see whales blowing almost every hour during the day." Or confirm Herman Melville's conviction of these graceful mammals' enduring greatness: "We account the whale immortal in his species, however perishable in his individuality. He swam the seas before the continents broke water; he once swam over the site of the Tuileries, and Windsor Castle, and the Kremlin. In Noah's flood he despised Noah's Ark; and if ever the world is to be again flooded, like the Netherlands, to kill off its rats, then the eternal whale will still survive, and rearing upon the topmost crest of the equatorial flood, spout his frothed defiance to the skies."

Nature's Odd Couple

We drove to Point Vicente on Palos Verdes Peninsula to look for gray whales. We came away even more impressed by a tiny butterfly, the El Segundo Blue. The large-bodied mammal swims thousands of miles a year to fulfill its life-cycle demands, whereas the El Segundo Blue goes nowhere, finding all its needs on a single plant rooted in the steep bluffs above the surging ocean through which the iconic whales annually migrate.

Neither strategy, it turns out, has been risk free.

Of the two, the gray whale is far better known; the timing and duration of its migration has captured the imagination of generations of those living on the Pacific Coast. Although the stuff of legend, its two-month-long voyage from its frigid feeding grounds in the Chukchi and Bering Seas to its southernmost bathtub-warm nursery in Baja's Magdalena Bay almost led to its extirpation.

Because eighteenth- and nineteenth-century whalers assiduously mapped the migration so they could murderously track gray whales as they plowed north and south, they were able to mount an indiscriminate slaughter of the slow-moving creatures. An estimated 8,000 adults, for example, were killed in and around Magdalena Bay between the mid-1840s and the mid-1870s, and thousands more calves died as a result of their mothers' destruction.

"No species of the whale tribe is so constantly and variously pursued," whaler Charles Scammon wrote in the *Proceedings of the Academy of Natural Sciences* in 1869. He should know, for he is credited with discovering their birthing grounds. Within a short period of time, these "large bays and lagoons where once these animals congregated, brought forth and nurtured their young, are now nearly deserted. Their mammoth bones lie bleaching on the shores of those placid waters." Because the "civilized hunter seeks the hunted animal farther seaward, as from year to year it learns to shun the fatal shore," before too long, he predicted, "the California gray will be known only as one of the extinct species of cetacea recorded in history."

Scammon's prediction almost came to be. That it did not, at least not in the eastern Pacific, was also due to the whales' round-trip migration, which served as the basis for conservationists' diligent efforts to protect these remarkable mammals from human predation.

In 1937, the League of Nations, and a decade later, the International Whaling Commission (IWC) established bans on the commercial hunting of gray whales; aboriginal subsistence hunting continues under IWC regulations. Additional protection emerged in the United States through the enactment of the Marine Mammal Protection

Act (1972) and the Endangered Species Act (1973), each of which listed the gray whale as an endangered species. Just as critical to the population's slow recovery has been the creation of a series of protected areas, such as the Channel Islands and Monterey Bay National Marine Sanctuaries, and the California Coastal National Monument lining its migratory route.

These institutionalized responses have gained considerable public support. That is because as the number of gray whales has rebounded to more than 20,000, it is now possible to see them in action. Whale sightseeing tours are launched from harbors everywhere, and observation sites have been built on such high ground as Point Vicente. There, with binoculars in hand, my wife and I joined a throng of people scattered along the well-trodden paths stretching north of the nearby lighthouse; all were scanning the blue horizon in hopes of spotting telltale signs—breach or spray—of whales in motion.

We saw only two grays on that clear, bright morning, but the fresh-aired experience was hardly a wash. While keeping a weather eye to sea, we came upon a series of informational signs that detailed the plight of the El Segundo Blue (ESB), a species that is indigenous to this high and dry land and about which we knew nothing.

Our ignorance is perhaps understandable, for no other butterfly on the planet flits so beneath the human imagination.

Consider the ESB's constrained life. Minute in size (its wing span is roughly one inch) and small in number (so endangered is it that since 1976 the Fish and Wildlife Service has declared it rare wherever found), it occupies a narrow range, the equally rare, undisturbed coastal dunes in Los Angeles and Santa Barbara Counties. During its short lifespan (adults last a few days, during which they mate, lay eggs, and die), it is also exclusive in niche, spending its entire life on the flowerheads of coast buckwheat (*Eriogonum parviflorum*—also known as dune or seacliff buckwheat). "The almost total involvement of all stages with a single plant part," argues researcher Rudolf Mattoni, "is unique among North American butterflies."

This uniqueness accounts for its near-undoing. Although humans have no economic interest in the El Segundo Blue, the same cannot be said for the windswept, sandy terrain within which it makes its home. Across the twentieth century, these dunes have proved a high-value commodity—as beachfront property for the rich, industrial sites for refineries, water-treatment facilities, power plants, and sand-mining operations, as well as waterfront commercial districts, roadways, and runways. Jets taking off from Los Angeles International Airport roll down tarmac that has buried prime ESB habitat; with liftoff, they thunder over its fragmented vestiges.

By the 1970s, with its habitat largely destroyed, the U.S. Fish and Wildlife Service stepped in, designating the ESB an endangered species in the very first cohort of listed butterflies. Yet its ecosystem had been so bulldozed—the urbanizing onslaught had already shrunk the El Segundo dune formations from an estimated 4.5 square miles (roughly 3,200 acres) to a series of minuscule islands in a wide concrete sea—that many conservationists wondered whether the insect was long for this earth.

Ironically enough, LAX, that most concretized space, was discovered to contain the largest ESB colony. Although less an acre of pristine dune remained there in the early 1990s, about 2,000 butterflies lived on a relatively undisturbed set of sixteen acres, home to more than 1,000 buckwheat. At the nearby Chevron refinery, 1.6 acres of dunes supported maybe four hundred ESB, and at Malaga Cove, at the base of Palos Verdes Peninsula, an even smaller colony of sixty or so had been observed. This was all that remained from what Mattoni calculated was the butterfly's historic population of 750,000 adults. A recent study suggests that its numbers may have soared to over 100,000, but even those gains mean that the ESB remains on the endangered list for a reason.

Its partial recovery is due to concerted human action. Like the indefatigable advocates for the protection of gray whales, the El Segundo Blue has its ardent champions. At the same time that the whale's fans were securing marine sanctuaries, the butterfly's proponents were adopting similar strategies, if on a much smaller scale. Encouraging the airport and other industrial sites voluntarily to set aside dunes on their properties, they sought to nudge beach cities to adopt new, more butterfly-friendly landscaping. The goal has been to replace the ubiquitous iceplant and other exotics with coast buckwheat, a process that over the past three decades has only slowly taken root.

One such conversion effort is visible along the Point Vincente Bluffs trail weaving through the Palos Verde Peninsula Conservancy; in 2005, the City of Rancho Palos Verdes designated the 1,200-acre site a nature preserve.

Although this site contained intact coastal bluff shrub and coastal cactus shrub habitats, it was thought to have been outside the El Segundo Blue's historic range—until, that is, scientists and citizens monitoring the bluffs and surrounding terrain discovered an ESB colony. Already committed to restoring the disturbed sectors, the conservancy received funding from the California Coastal Commission to remove exotic and invasive plants and revegetate with buckwheat and other natives (a biota that will also support the Palos Verde Blue butterfly and such threatened bird species as the California gnatcatcher and coastal cactus wren).

The work continues, signaling the conservancy's sustained effort to return this small patch of land to its former health and to reinvigorate its biodiversity. Yet for this laudable project to succeed will depend on factors now mostly beyond human control, not least of which is time itself. So thoroughly and for so long have we run roughshod over ESB habitat that the butterfly's future, Mattoni warned in 1992, was "grim," a prognosis that has not changed substantively.

Still, one could have predicted the same about the gray whale's slim chance of survival (as whaler Scammon once did), so its recovery offers some optimism about the El Segundo Blue's fate—a hope revived whenever the graceful and bulky mammal rounds Point Vicente and breaks through the Pacific's shimmering surface.

Shifting Tide

"Ot-ter! Ot-ter!" That may not have been our daughter's first word, but it was among her most excited.

We had just walked into the Monterey Bay Aquarium and had made our way through the crowd to the sea otter exhibit when we were transfixed by the mammal's liquid grace, its corkscrewing motion through the pool. As it spun, dove, and curled up and around, we explained to our riveted two-year-old what we were looking at and pronounced the animal's name. That's when she let loose: "Ot-ter! Ot-ter!"

Memories of her exuberant cry surfaced in mid-December 2013 when news came that the Fish and Wildlife Service had abandoned its twenty-five-year-old ban on southern sea otters (*Enhydra lutris nereis*) residing in Southern California's waters. The ban, an outgrowth of the Reagan administration's aggressive antienvironmentalism, proved once more that if given a chance nature can make a mockery of command-and-control policymaking.

That is not to say that humans are incapable of pushing a species to the brink of extinction (and beyond). The otter almost became, like the passenger pigeon, a byword in North American environmental annals, a once-prolific species that market hunters wiped out.

The crux of the matter is the marine mammal's luxuriant pelt, a water-resistant fur that contains upwards of 650,000 hairs per square inch, thick insulation necessary for the frigid Pacific waters it calls home. "These animals are very beautiful," observed Georg Wilhelm Steller of the St. Petersburg Imperial Academy of Sciences in *The Beasts of the Sea* (1751). Because of their beauty, he wrote, "they are very valuable, as one may well believe of a skin the hairs of which, an inch or an inch and a half in length, are very soft, very thickly set, jet black and glossy." The German-born naturalist, who studied and hunted sea otters across the northern Pacific, concluding that the species "was incomparable, without a peer; it surpasses all other inhabitants of the vast ocean, and holds the first rank in point of beauty and softness of its fur."

Other eighteenth-century Russian expeditions, as well as those the English and Spanish mounted, shared Steller's calculation that this fur-rich creature had an unparalleled market value, triggering a grisly trade. At least initially, sea otters were relatively easy to kill. "They were found there in so great abundance that from the beginning our numbers did not suffice to kill them," Steller recounts about his experience on Bering Island. "They covered the shore in great droves, and as the animal is not migratory, but is born and bred there, they are so far from fearing man that they would come up to our fires and would not be driven away until, after many of them had been slain, they learned to know us and run away."

After wiping out the otters in the Bering Sea, Russian hunters ventured into the Aleutian Islands in the 1740s; there, not incidentally, they also brutalized the Aleut people so they could accelerate their harvest of otters. The payoff seemed to sanction their vicious fury. In the late 1770s, for instance, Captain James Cook's crew killed a number of sea otters in southeastern Alaska and later sold the pelts in Canton for an estimated 1,800 percent profit. The news spread rapidly, and the slaughter began in earnest.

American vessels shipping out of Boston joined the pursuit of the sea otter, ultimately dominating the exploitation. By the late 1810s, the mammal had been cleaned out of Alaska and much of the coast south to San Francisco Bay. By that time, American fur hunters were annually killing thousands of otters around the Farallon Islands, and so brutally efficient were they that they extirpated the resident population within a decade.

The killing fields shifted south, with the same bloody result. By 1835, when Richard Henry Dana came ashore in San Diego during his two years before the mast, the pickings were slim. He and his mates packed the *Pilgrim*'s hold with tens of thousands of cowhides and horns, and a scant few barrels of otter and seal fur. Within a half century of Cook's expedition, the southern sea otter no longer occupied its kelp-forest habitat along the Pacific

Coast, from Alaska to Mexico; as best anyone knew, it was gone forever.

Naturally, only after being decimated did the sea otter receive a modest form of international protection. It was among the fur-bearing mammals that fell under the protective arm of the 1911 Convention between the United States and Other Powers Providing for the Preservation and Protection of Fur Seals, an awkwardly named treaty that contained narrow regulatory aspirations.

Its chief promoter was conservationist and artist Henry Wood Elliot, author of *Our Arctic Province: Alaska and the Seal Islands* (1886), a text that especially focused on the stellar landscapes, indigenous peoples, and unusual wildlife in the then little-known region. Convinced that rigorously enforced regulations on seal and otter hunting would bring back their once-bounteous numbers, in 1905 Elliott encouraged U.S. Secretary of State John Hay to coauthor a proposal that six years later served as the basis for the international treaty.

Its provisions, to which Great Britain, Russia, and Japan were the other signatories, granted the United States sole authority to ban pelagic hunting and manage the onshore killing on the Bering Sea's Pribilof Islands, and granted aboriginal peoples the right to harvest animals for domestic consumption (that is, for noncommercial purposes). Washington's first step was to announce a five-year moratorium on all hunting to allow the seal and otter populations to stabilize, and for the next thirty years the federal government granted hunters access to the islands and established minimum "takes" of these fur-bearing mammals.

Although landmark legislation—it was the first international treaty to regulate such exploitation and is credited with establishing a precedent for the Fur Seal Act of 1966, which established the Pribilofs as a "special reservation" for the protection of these endangered mammals, and the 1972 Marine Mammal Protection Act that prohibited, with a few exceptions, the killing of threatened and endangered marine mammals in U.S. waters—the 1911 treaty had no real impact on the southern sea otter. After all, they had been exterminated.

Or so everyone thought. Then, in 1938, a small colony was found along the remote Big Sur coast, living in and around the mouth of Bixby Creek. From this group of fifty, the southern sea otter population has rebounded in fits and starts. Forty years on, it amounted to more than 1,000 animals and in 1977 was formally listed as "threatened" under the Endangered Species Act; this designation offered it protection under federal law and led to considerable research into its life history, habitat requirements, and prospects for recovery.

Such essential ecological work received a major boost after the Monterey Bay Aquarium opened its doors in 1984: Its researchers and curators developed exhibits and informational guides that deepened the knowledge of its millions of visitors about the sea otters' plight (and that of other endangered species that inhabit the central California coast). Our daughter was not alone in her enthusiastic response to these remarkably resilient creatures. "Charismatic, furry, and cute," observes historian Connie Y. Chiang in *Shaping the Shoreline: Fisheries and Tourism on the Monterey Coast*, "they became the aquarium's closest thing to a 'celebrity' species."

However celebrated, its newfound status did not protect the sea otter as it slowly began to repopulate its former territory from Santa Barbara to the south. The Reagan administration, eager to roll back environmental protections that a bipartisan coalition of earlier presidents and Congresses had enacted, intervened to restrict its southerly migration. Responding swiftly to complaints from commercial shellfisheries that the sea otter, whose diet includes sea urchins, crustaceans, and mollusks, was in direct competition with their operations, it pushed the Fish and Wildlife Service to resolve the dispute in industry's favor.

The agency complied, and in 1986 declared an otter-free zone stretching from the U.S.-Mexico Border to Point Conception, north of Santa Barbara. The only space within this zone that otters could find sanctuary was on San Nicholas Island, which lies within the political jurisdiction of Ventura County but which the U.S. Navy controls as a weapons testing and training facility. All others, if captured, would be relocated outside Southern California.

Otters paid little attention to the niceties of this political compromise; apparently they don't read the Federal
Registry, where its conditions were posted. Instead they
continued to swim south in search of food, shelter, and
mates. Those that survived relocation to the central coast,
and not all did, headed south once more.

It took time, and a more favorable political climate, to
rescind the flawed 1986 otter-free-zone ruling. In August
2011, the Fish and Wildlife Service proposed removing the
regulations that governed the movement of the southern
sea otter because "the southern sea otter translocation
program has failed to fulfill its purpose," acknowledging,
too, that "our recovery and management goals for the
species cannot be met by continuing the program." After
fourteen months of public comment, hearings, and evalu-
ation, on December 19, 2012, the federal agency officially
stopped enforcing the unenforceable regulation, allowing
"southern sea otters to expand their range naturally into
southern California waters."

Reestablishing themselves will not be easy. There
is the potential for deadly interactions with commercial
shellfish operators, as has happened even in protected preserves. Throughout its current range, moreover, infectious
diseases and viruses, among other debilities, are caus-
ing a higher level of mortality than had been predicted,
inhibiting population growth, a pattern that may well continue as sea otters press into the Southland. Their survival
will be compromised further by the very waters through

which they will swim: the effluent that streams into Santa Monica Bay, out of San Pedro and Long Beach harbors, and from the many polluted rivers and creeks that flow into the Pacific, will undercut their life chances.

Despite these and other obstacles, I would not bet against this compact, powerful, and well-groomed mammal. After all, sea otters somehow have survived in the face of more than a century of human exploitation. So if someday soon you spot one or two cavorting among kelp rafts off Malibu, Palos Verdes, or Crystal Cove, you'll know what to shout: Ot-ter! Ot-ter!

Monumental Seashore

President Obama's 2014 State of the Union speech contained lots of promises. They were not all fulfilled, of course, but one of them, only hinted at in his address, was realized shortly thereafter.

The intimation was tucked into a paragraph focused on how America was achieving greater energy independence and why natural gas was "the bridge fuel that can power our economy with less of the carbon pollution that causes climate change." Obama's closing thought was a seemingly offhand remark: "And while we're at it, I'll use my authority to protect more of our pristine federal lands for future generations."

Those provocative words may have slipped below many people's radar, but to activists pressing the president to use the Antiquities Act (1906) to set aside additional wildlands, they were an executive elixir. Because the act empowers Obama to designate new or expand the limits of current national monuments without congressional oversight—a privilege Theodore Roosevelt, Jimmy Carter, and Bill Clinton used repeatedly—the signal seemed clear. The preservation of more scenic and significant landscapes was in the offing.

Among those cheering this prospect were a committed group of citizens in Mendocino County. For nearly three years they had been urging that the Stornetta Public Lands, a 1,665-acre rugged tract fronting the Pacific that the Bureau of Land Management (BLM) stewarded, become part of the California Coastal National Monument. Such an inclusion, they reasoned, made sense on environmental grounds. Although the BLM would continue to oversee the property, the site would gain greater protection with the new designation. It also would have a beneficial economic impact, luring an increasing number of visitors to southern Mendocino, a stimulus to local commerce.

They now have a chance to test those propositions: in March 2014, at a small White House ceremony, President Obama signed the order that folded the Stornetta property into the national monument. With the stroke of his pen, he made the gateway town of Port Arena (pop. 449) a very happy place. "People are just ecstatic," Ann Cole, executive director of the Mendocino Land Trust, told the *Santa Rosa Press Democrat.* "They've been working so hard on this."

Obama's invocation of the Antiquities Act is a partial consequence of Inside-the-Beltway gridlock. The House of Representatives had unanimously approved the relevant bill that local representative Jared Huffman (D-Marin) had introduced in 2013, but its paired legislation in the Senate, which Barbara Boxer and Dianne Feinstein had authored, had not yet come to the floor.

By acting in advance of the legislative branch, the administration hoped to bolster its environmental credibility. Mike Matz, who directs the U.S. public lands program at the Pew Charitable Trusts, suggested as much to the *Washington Post*: "The fact that the President is willing to exercise his authority is more than symbolic. It's a step toward more balance between protection and development. And, if Congress gets into a healthy competition with him over which branch can do more, all the better."

That land-protection rush is highly unlikely to occur anytime soon, given the very partisan split in Congress that gave the president the leeway he thought he needed to use the Antiquities Act.

Indeed, the situation on Capitol Hill at that time was not dissimilar to that governing the political landscape Bill Clinton occupied in 2000 when he employed the Antiquities Act to set aside the California Coastal National Monument in the first place; it is telling that John Podesta, one of President Obama's counselors, was among Clinton's advisers urging him to sign off on the original enabling legislation.

Whatever the backroom wheeling and dealing, Clinton and Obama did right. The now-expanded national monument covers eleven hundred miles of some of the world's most spectacular coastline and offshore features. Running north from Mexico to Oregon, it comprises thousands of islands, exposed reefs, pinnacles, and seastacks, marine habitat that is home to such pelagic species as pelicans, murres, cormorants, gulls, petrels, and auklets. There they are joined by elephant seals and at least two threatened species, the California otter and the Stellar's sea lion. A passing parade of gray whales, on their migration south and north, moves through the monument's chilled waters, and the tidal pools are a treasure trove of life.

The Stornetta addition adds to these botanical riches. Key among its contributions is the Garcia River estuary, which the BLM has identified as critical habitat for Coho and Chinook salmon, and for the Point Arena mountain beaver, Behren's silver spot butterfly, western snowy plover, and California red-legged frog. Adding immense aesthetic value are the wind- and tide-carved bluffs, promontories offering a visual and aural feast of brilliant sunsets, barking seals, and the wash of water on rock.

Why this stretch of spectacular coastline was redesignated in advance of the 1.4 million acres in Utah dubbed Greater Canyonlands that surrounds Canyon-lands National Park is a matter not of its ecological integrity but of political divisiveness. As Secretary of the Interior Sally Jewell observed several times before and after her visit to Point Arena, the Obama administration's calculus for Antiquities Act designations depended on local community buy-in and across-the-aisle support.

Mendocino County was able to demonstrate the necessary unity, helped in no small measure by its location in a solidly Democratic district in a solidly Democratic state.

The other proposed landscapes, for all their many natural virtues, are in regions where environmental preservation is a deeply contested, and often reviled, principle. President Obama has had no interest in reigniting the kind of destructive furor that erupted in Utah in 1996 after Bill Clinton announced the creation of Grand Staircase–Escalante National Monument and that continues to fuel Sagebrush Rebellion activism, including the legislative and gubernatorial legal gambits to take over all federal lands in the Beehive State.

To wish that things were different is to wish that evocative language about nature's integrity could mute partisan discourse and the hyperbole on which it depends—to hope that we can listen to how words sound about places we love and, by immersing ourselves in their galvanizing essence, be persuaded to act in these wildlands' defense. Such a sensibility is announced in the opening words to Clinton's proclamation creating the California Coastal National Monument: "The islands, rocks, and pinnacles . . . overwhelm the viewer, as white-capped waves crash into the vertical cliffs or deeply crevassed surge channels and frothy water empties back into the ocean."

In this surge—relentless, enduring, and powerful—lies our charge.

Murrelet Power

For such a tiny thing, the marbled murrelet packs a wallop. The timber industry has learned this the hard way. In late February 2015 it lost yet another lawsuit that it hoped would strip the robin-sized bird of its threatened-species status, opening the way for the clear-cutting of old-growth coastal forests in California, Oregon, and Washington. The DC District Court of Appeals rejected the appeal, marking the loggers' fifth straight defeat at the hands—well, really, webbed feet—of the murrelet.

The pelagic bird's legal clout has depended on its unusual uniting of ocean and forest. Although murre-lets spend most of their life swimming on, winging over, and fishing from the Pacific's cold waters, when it comes time to give birth they head for ancient hemlock and redwood, Sitka spruce, and Douglas fir. They nest only in these towering sentinels, laying a single egg in these trees' moss-covered branches, sites that can be as much as fifty miles inland from where waves crash on rocky shore. Grind these pine-scented forests into sawdust and the murrelet disappears from this part of its historic range.

It was a tree trimmer, aptly enough, who is often credited with discovering the tight connection between the murrelet's nesting behavior and its arboreal home ground. One day in early August 1974, Hoyt Foster was scaling up a 212-foot Douglas fir in Big Basin Redwood State Park in the Santa Cruz Mountains. About 150 above the forest floor, as Foster was ready to plant his foot on a mossy branch, he looked down and spotted a murrelet chick. At least according to the scientific record, this was the first time that anyone had come upon a nesting site, thus clearing up a mystery of where and how murrelets gave birth that had baffled observers for nearly two centuries.

What these researchers realized quickly was that the canny seabird chose mature and old-growth trees because only these had branches wide enough to balance their eggs on; only these trees were tall enough to keep their young above predators—natural predators, in any event. Humans posed another kind of threat, for the very species most suited to murrelet reproduction and species regeneration were the ones that loggers yearned to cut into board feet and truck to market.

But it is not the murrelet that is usually associated with the great timber wars that blew up in the Pacific Northwest in the 1970s and that continued until the mid-1990s. The spotted owl and salmon—which also depend on healthy old-growth forest ecosystems—were at the center of that furious controversy. The number of lawsuits filed on these species' behalf, like the countless local, regional, and national organizations that sided with the endangered raptor and fish, were countered by a coalition of timber industry associations and millworkers, public representatives, and community officials.

This brawl slowly, painfully died down after the Clinton administration's 1994 Northwest Forest Plan; it sharply reduced the use of clear-cutting and the amount of wood harvested on the U.S. National Forests in the region. Noted Jack Ward Thomas, who would become the chief of the U.S. Forest Service as a result of his leading the interdisciplinary research team that established the scientific basis for its provisions: "President Clinton had, if nothing else, stepped into a vacuum and made a decision."

This act—and the ecosystem-based management on which it was based—immediately found favor in the federal court system. In the words of Judge William Dwyer in 1994: "Given the current state of the forests, there is no way that agencies can comply with environmental laws without planning on an ecosystem basis." The implications for spotted owl and salmon were clear. Their habitat must be protected as the default; management plans must revolve around their needs.

Though not mentioned in this decision, the murrelet benefited as a result of this contentious environment and the judicial decisions it produced. One reason for this emerged on the Siuslaw National Forest, located along the central Oregon coast. Since the post–World War II period, it had been one of, if not the, most productive forest in the national system—if productivity is measured simply in terms of the amount of wood harvested. Timber management there "mirrored industrial forestry," its former supervisor, Jim Furnish, wrote in his memoir, *Toward a Natural Forest* (2015). As its managers liquidated old growth and replanted a monoculture of Douglas fir, as they sprayed herbicides and fertilizers, the "Siuslaw spent more money per acre than any other national forest because it generated the most wood and revenue per acre."

These economic benefits ran right into an interrelated set of ecological deficits for which Furnish and his peers along the northern Pacific Coast had to account: steep declines in spotted owl and salmon populations, as well as troubling data about timber harvesting's impact on the marbled murrelet. By the late 1990s, federal and state scientists assessing murrelet behavior ranging from the Santa Cruz Mountains north into Oregon had concluded that breeding murrelets exhibit site fidelity—that is, they return year after year to the same nesting area. As such, if a nesting stand is logged off, these particular birds may not breed again.

On the Siuslaw, for example, the data revealed that "nine out of ten mature timber stands had nesting owls and murrelets—which meant no more timber harvest." What Furnish and his leadership team concluded was that "this incredibly productive landscape could not simultaneously maximize timber products and wildlife."

Because these redwood, spruce, and fir forests were "the womb that sustained this natural abundance," and because by law this abundance itself must be sustained, "the remaining mature forest in the Coastal Range would stay standing."

In an effort to undo this principled reasoning, the timber industry has been trying to delist the marbled murrelet as a threatened species, stripping it of its protections and opening the way for a return of clear-cutting. "The timber industry continues to take the narrow, regressive view," Furnish has written, "that the Endangered Species Act simply doesn't matter."

In this particular case, *American Forest Research Council v. Ashe* (13-5302), the court was asked to determine whether marbled murrelets inhabiting California, Oregon, and Washington were a "distinct population segment" from other species living in Canada and Alaska; if the court found that the U.S. Fish and Wildlife Service had erred in identifying it as "discrete in relation to the remainder of its species," then it would have erred as well in listing it as threatened. The court concluded otherwise, offering evidence of the population's discreteness that is in fact quite damning of the renewed-harvesting ambitions that led to the timber industry's lawsuit: "(1) the murrelet population in the U.S. is one-third the size of that of Canada; (2) the productivity of murrelets is lower in the U.S. than Canada; (3) the loss of murrelet habitat (old-growth forest) in recent years has been more severe in the

U.S. than Canada; and (4) the absolute amount of murrelet nesting habitat is smaller in the U.S. than Canada."

Given these distinctions, and in light of other confirming evidence, the court shut down this latest attempt to undercut the marbled murrelet's life chances along the Pacific Northwest coast. In doing so, it also gave the coastal forests an opportunity to recover in tandem with the diminutive seabird they have long nurtured.

Pulling Back

A rueful smile. That's how the desk clerk at the Sea Otter Motel in Cambria, California, reacted when asked if she could tell us when the northern elephant seals (*Mirounga angustirostris*) first took up residence on Piedras Blancas beach, just north of San Simeon on the state's Central Coast. She didn't hesitate, dating her awareness to a winter's afternoon in the late 1980s when her dog stank to high heaven.

She and her labrador had headed to the beach that day for a little R&R. The owner read; the dog ran. But after a lengthy lope along the wide, curving strand, the black lab came back reeking. Unable to identify its source, its owner walked down the beach and was startled to come upon on a small group of elephant seals—and suspected her pet had rolled in their poop. As for the nose-wrinkling stench: for the next half hour, she flung a tennis ball into the cold surf for her dog to fetch, letting the churning saltwater wash it off.

Although hers sounds like a shaggy dog tale, researchers tracking the elephant seal population along the Central Coast confirm that these large mammals began to recolonize Piedras Blancas around that time. Their return to this beach, and their lumbering, roaring presence on it, is a striking example of the interplay between two drivers—exploitation and stewardship—that so often define human relations with the natural world.

Mayhem initially took precedence. Beginning in the late eighteenth century, European and American whalers began to cruise the Pacific Coast, from Baja California to British Columbia; during their winter voyages, they found vast colonies of elephant seals located on countless rocky islands and coastal beaches. Those cooler months are when the seals haul out of the ocean and females give birth to pups conceived eleven months earlier. Even as this new generation is being weaned, dominant males impregnate harems of females; shortly thereafter the seals disperse, launching a migratory foraging that lasts until the next winter.

Hunters were just as habituated to these breeding grounds, returning each year to slaughter thousands of animals for their oil. Pursuing them with the same ferocity leveled against the sperm whale (*Physeter macrocephalus*), sealers decimated the northern elephant seal population. An 1868 report about the Baja killing fields testifies to how thorough this bloody harvest could be: "In some years there have been reported to have been not less than thirty whaling and sealing camps below San Diego, aggregating some 2,000 men; and as seals and the affiliate families are in the greatest abundance, cargoes [are] often prepared with great rapidity."

Within a few years, the animal was presumed extinct. Then in 1892 a Smithsonian Institution expedition spotted eight adults on Guadalupe Island off Baja—and promptly killed seven of them. Somehow enough seals remained undetected to maintain some semblance of viability. By 1922, a joint Mexican-U.S. research team counted 264 seals on Guadalupe, at which point Mexico took action. That same year it passed legislation making it illegal to kill or capture elephant seals, even stationing a small garrison on the waterless isle to protect its remnant population.

From this principled intervention has emerged one of the great mammalian recovery stories. The progeny of Guadalupe's seals soon enough sought out one-time breeding sites on nearby islands off the Baja coast. As they spread northward to the Channel Islands, which they reached by the 1950s, they received U.S. protection via such international treaties as the Convention on Nature Protection and Wild Life Preservation in the Western Hemisphere (1940), and later the Marine Mammal Protection Act (1972) and the Endangered Species Act (1973). Twenty years later, northern elephant seals had reclaimed breeding territory on the Farallon Islands, and researchers estimated that the total population had soared to nearly 50,000.

That a decade or so later individuals began to come ashore along California's Central Coast thus makes sense. So did these animals' selection of Piedras Blancas beach, a cozy sweep of sand protected from fierce Pacific winter storms by Piedras Blancas Point; entangling kelp forests offshore help keep such predators as orcas and great white sharks at bay. This is an almost ideal locale to ensure seal pups' chances of survival.

They have done more than survive, proliferating at an astonishing rate: in 1990, less than two dozen populated a small cove hugging the point that one year later held more than 400. In 1992, the first known pup was birthed on the beach, a number that swelled to 600 in 1995. The next year upwards of 1,000 were brought to life in the prolific colony that now sprawled for miles, including a stretch bordering the Pacific Coast Highway.

That's where we joined a mid-January crowd of people strolling along the wooden boardwalk and pressing against the fence-line that paralleled a twenty-foot bluff overlooking the rookery. Below, alpha males threatened rivals by sound and movement; when a nasal bellow did not work, chase ensued; they brooked no opposition. Females flipped sand on their backs to shield them from the sun's warmth and barked at cagey interlopers seeking to oust them from their ground. Pups squawked to be fed, nudging their mothers' abdomens in search of a milky nipple. Leaning over the rail to get a closer look at the noisy herd, a young girl marveled: "There's tons of them."

She's right, but whether this robust pinniped population is sustainable is another matter. Ecologists are concerned that the northern elephant seals' genetic past might catch up with them. The current population—now estimated at more than 150,000—traces its ancestry to that tiny group of surviving seals on Guadalupe Island. As few as two breeding bulls could be the source of its paternal gene pool, a worrisome outcome that may hinder this species's adaptability to a climate-disrupted environment.

In question, too, is whether elephant seals will adapt to a variety of human pressures. Agricultural effluent and urban runoff have compromised the health of a number of other marine species, seals included, an impact that will increase as populations surge. Direct conflicts with humans may also intensify. The more territory elephant seals occupy, the more likely they'll oust surfers and sunbathers from once-prized beaches; their larger presence has already increased the sightings of the seals' predators in the waters we sail, swim, and paddle. How these and other tensions will be managed is open to question.

Some answers are available at Piedras Blancas beach. As its rookery exploded in size, a local grassroots group, Friends of the Elephant Seal, quickly formed. It became an invaluable educational forum; its docents daily offer advice to visitors about the seals' life cycle, their habits and habitat, with the goal of building greater awareness of and support for the species's continued presence here and elsewhere.

Their onshore activism has been sustained via federal and state management of the marine environment. The Monterey Bay National Marine Sanctuary, which the National Oceanic and Atmospheric Administration oversees, stretches from Cambria north to Marin County and incorporates this rookery; a series of overlapping state-designated Marine Protected Areas also lie offshore of Piedras Blancas beach, and the powerful California Coastal Commission keeps a close watch over this site, so altogether there's a raft of essential regulatory oversight.

These voluntary actions and legislative initiatives embody a healthy humility, allowing these animals we nearly extirpated the chance to reclaim their historic range. Giving way is how we can give back.

Fiery Terrain

The Fire Next Time

A wildland fire is never just a fire. Even as it burns through forests, grasslands, or chaparral, it also eats into the political landscape, like acid on a copper plate. And in that etching, with the surface opened up, we can glimpse a society's most basic philosophical commitments, its deepest operating assumptions. Underscoring this point is the Wallow Fire, the largest during summer 2011.

It erupted on that May 29, perhaps after campers abandoned a still-hot campfire in the Bear Wallow Wilderness on the Apache-Sitgreaves National Forest in eastern Arizona; from that small ignition point, it raced outward to become the single largest in the state's history. During its harrowing month-long run, and fueled by strong winds, scorching temperatures, and microscopic levels of humidity, the Wallow blackened more than 538,000 acres, roughly 841 square miles. (As a point of comparison, the monstrous 2009 Station Fire in the San Gabriel Mountains of Southern California took out 250 square miles.)

Its size and devastation aside—and notwithstanding the tremendous smoke column it produced, which stretched all the way to the Great Lakes, befouling the

Middle West's air quality—the most striking thing about the Wallow was its lightning speed. To get a sense for how fast it blew up, the *Arizona Republic* created a kinetic map that highlighted the firestorm's rapid expansion based in part on its ability to hurl embers upwards of five to six miles in advance of its frontlines, igniting troublesome spot fires. It is no wonder it took firefighters so long to contain the Wallow Fire's energy; no wonder that in this lightly populated region more than sixty-five hundred people had to flee for their lives.

Yet few of these evacuees lost their homes; only thirty-two were destroyed and but five damaged. That low number seems inconsistent with the hyperventilating reporting that occurred during the fire's top-of-the-fold status in that June's news cycle. Print and electronic media could not get enough of the story.

I can still hear the snap-crackle-pop of hundred-foot flames that torched stand after stand, an admittedly terrifying sound that seemed to transfix the nightly anchors. I can still picture, lumbering overhead, the converted DC-10 (its ingenuous acronym is VLAT = Very Large Air Tanker), which carried a 12,000-gallon payload of orange-red fire retardant: released in hopes of slowing down the fire's surge, the brilliantly colored liquid offered up a telegenic moment if ever there was one; CNN was seduced, endlessly looping this bit of pyro porn.

How was it possible, then, given this obsession with the aural and visual sensations of destruction, that there was relatively little damage to the towns that dot the eastern extent of the White Mountains?

Take a look at what happened to Alpine, Arizona. Perfectly named—the high valley its 256 residents call home sits at an elevation of 8,050 feet—the town is completely surrounded by the Apache-Sitgreaves. So when Jim Aylor, the fire management officer of the Alpine Fire District, looked up and saw the holocaust racing from tree crown to tree crown, he had every right to be worried, very worried. "The smoke column was bent over making it difficult to see," he recalled. But it was what he heard that was most ominous: as the fire roared "over the ridge toward Alpine it sounded like a freight train."

It never arrived. Instead, on the town's outskirts the fire dropped to the ground, slowing its speed of spread, which allowed firefighters to knock down the flames even as the main body of the fire swept around the community to incinerate the enveloping wooded terrain to the north and south. However miraculous this may seem, it was no miracle: Alpine was spared because of human intervention.

Homeowners in the preceding years, with the guidance of and funding from state and federal forestry agencies, had created defensible space around their property; they cleared away the understory, thinned trees, and built homes that were "firewise" to decrease the amount of fuel available to stoke wildland fires such as the Wallow. In the immediate days and hours before the fiery surge leaped into view, hot-shot crews also had conducted extensive backfiring operations that proved critical to the town's defense.

The single most important strategic move had occurred some years earlier, a consequence of the 2003 Healthy Forest Restoration Act (HFRA: PL 108-148). Congress had enacted the legislation to promote the thinning of forests close to human settlement due to the intensely damaging fire season of the preceding summer and fall, when more than 88,000 separate wildfires burned about 7 million acres. One of them, the 2002 Rodeo-Chediski, also tore through the Apache-Sitgreaves; it destroyed hundreds of homes, cooked more than 450,000 acres, and earned the dubious distinction of being Arizona's largest conflagration until the Wallow.

The Healthy Forest initiative, despite its commitment to increasing fire safety in the combustible West, has not been controversy-free. A number of environmental organizations challenged its provisions in court, believing that it would intensify timber production in the national forests and allow the Forest Service to ignore environmental regulations; the Ninth Circuit Court of Appeals, whose jurisdiction covers the Far West states, agreed. In *Sierra Club v. Bosworth* (2007), it rebuked the agency for excluding some small projects from filing environmental impact statements, a decision it believed was "arbitrary and capricious."

For the residents of Alpine, there was nothing random or fickle about the Forest Service spending HFRA-authorized dollars via innovative fuels-treatment programs known as the White Mountain Stewardship Contract and the Four Forest Restoration Initiative. Since 2004, the agency annually has treated 50,000 acres, a good portion of which are located in and around the mountain towns of Alpine, Greer, Springfield, and Nutrioso, all points on the map that became highly visible when the national media aimed its telephoto lens on the Wallow's wrath.

As became evident in postfire photographs, the fuels-treatment teams had chosen their plots carefully and done their work well; in Alpine, the fire lay down when it hit the thinned woods, exactly as desired; narrating this process is the shifting color of the trees, shading from charred black to vivid green.

Although not all of the treated units worked equally well, in a larger sense they were an unequivocal success. Our national investment saved these towns; they still stand because we stood with them.

This declaration of interdependence, this assertion of the demonstrable benefits that come from a binding social compact, has been attacked routinely by members of the so-called Tea Party. Yet as the Wallow Fire illuminates, this partisan assault on the essential role that government can play in our lives could not be more ill-conceived or poorly timed. That's because more and more Americans are moving into the wildland-urban interface, increasing pressure on firefighting agencies at a time of politically motivated and irresponsible budget cuts.

That message is as relevant to Arizona, whose state politics are dominated by staunch conservatives, as it is in California, which could not be more blue. Its Southern California mountain communities of Big Bear, Lake Arrowhead, and Idyllwild, Mount Baldy Village and Wrightwood, are as vulnerable as Alpine. Around each of these high-elevation towns, and to different degrees, fuels-treatment projects have been completed; one of them already proved its worth during the 2003 Old Fire, which threatened, but did not burn, a North Lake Arrowhead resort area; nearly 3,000 homes were thereby protected.

But not enough has been done due to the hefty price tag that accompanies forest-health restoration projects. The high costs are as much a result of demography as of finance. The Southland's massive population means that tens of thousands of visitors head up into the local mountains for rest and relaxation almost every day of the week. The reality of their swelling presence, and the dense built landscape that has been constructed to meet their needs— upwards of 100,000 structures crowd the mountain lakes district of the San Bernardino Mountains—complicates the use of prescribed burning and mechanical treatments to clear the thickening undergrowth.

That landscape needs judicious cutting, too. The Southern California forests contain so much drought-induced dead or dying vegetation, arguably the greatest die-off in the country, that the idea of "thinning" this stock is baffling: Where would you start? Where stop? And once the logs are cut, what would you do with them in a region that has no lumber mills?

These questions help explain why the treatment costs in the San Bernardino and San Gabriel Mountains are astronomical. In 2003, the average was approximately $4,000 per acre, which four years later had been lowered to $2,000. Even that drop in price remains well above the national average, which is why without a sustained infusion of funds, these mountain towns are at considerable risk.

Their vulnerability will not be reduced anytime soon, for the political will needed to secure the essential funding for communities scattered across the forested regions of the Inland Empire or the Intermountain West is distressingly lacking.

To get the necessary dollars will require a very different electorate, a very different Congress. Rather than committing ourselves to the commonweal, to one another, contemporary Republican fantasies of buccaneering individualism prevail. Instead of bolstering our governing commitments with dedicated (and robust) fiscal resources, we get a corrosive right-wing budget "compromise" that has gutted core governmental services we cannot afford to lose.

If you need a refresher course on what a conscientious government can accomplish with and for its people, study Alpine, Arizona. It is a symbol of hope in this dispiriting moment in American history. It would be nice if voters and their representatives would embrace the message conveyed in that small town's salvation before the next wind-whipped inferno comes thundering over the ridge.

Lesson Learned?

Angelenos cannot stop talking about the 2009 Station Fire. With reason: when an arsonist ignited it on August 26, no one could know that it would continue to burn until mid-October; that it would kill two valiant firefighters, torch upwards of one hundred structures, and consume 160,000 acres of the Angeles National Forest, blackening much of the San Gabriel Mountains. Or that it would become the largest fire to date in Los Angeles County, and the most costly.

Its aftermath has been as incendiary. Even as firefighters struggled to gain control of the blaze, even as its thick, dark smoke still churned skyward, creating its own microclimate, criticism erupted. Why had it taken so long for the Forest Service to gain traction in the fight? What decisions had led to the grounding of the federal agency's air fleet in the crucial first night of the fire? Why, homeowners wondered, had they lost their homes—was it a result of command-and-control failures? And were communication glitches the reason two Los Angeles County firefighters lost their lives on Mount Gleason?

The questions continued to pile up in the ensuing years and the local media continued to pile on. Representative Adam Schiff (D-Pasadena) proved particularly persistent in his inquiries, holding a number of well-covered public hearings locally and in Washington, DC, that probed the Forest Service's responses to the fire and its postfire analyses of what went wrong; he demanded a Department of Agriculture, Office of Inspector-General accounting of the federal land-management agency's actions and inactions, a 2011 report that neither exonerated nor excoriated the Forest Service. Schiff was also indefatigable in his calls for the agency to update its policies governing nighttime flying operations (which it has done; unlike 2009, under certain conditions fire-retardant-carrying fixed-wing aircraft and helicopters now may stay airborne after dark).

Schiff's prevailing hypothesis, which the *Los Angeles Times* and a host of other media outfits mirrored, was that Forest Service incident commanders immediately should have thrown all mechanical and human resources at the Station Fire; had they done so, he predicted, the conflagration would not have blown up to such immense, terrifying, and deadly proportions.

The fact that this fire blew up had to be someone's fault, and the blame for it lay squarely on the shoulders of the federal agency.

Although such after-the-fact interrogations are as critical as they are routinized, and Representative Schiff did what an engaged and responsible public official should do on behalf of his constituency, some troubling consequences grew out of these inquiries and complicated the future fire management on the public lands. These ramifications, however unintended, must also be acknowledged if we are to have a full and accurate understanding of the Station Fire's impact on firefighting policy.

Recall, for example, what happened the next summer when a trio of small fires popped up in Kern and Los Angeles Counties. No sooner had the Bull, West, and Crown blazed forth in late July 2010 than CalFire (the state agency), the Forest Service, and local fire departments rushed as much personnel and equipment that they could muster to suppress them; thousands of firefighters and squadrons of aircraft and bulldozers were dispatched to put down the wind-driven, fast-moving grass fires.

Lesson learned, one could argue—and many did. But the massive show of strength (underscored by then-governor Arnold Schwarzenegger's weight-lifting photo-op and his chiseled appearance at command headquarters for the West Fire) deflected attention away from another set of questions that ought to have been raised in response to the quick marshalling of resources.

Not all fires must be controlled; some are essential to maintain ecosystem health. Not all firefighting makes economic sense, either. Yes, the commitment to protect human life is nonnegotiable, the swift punishment of arsonists is essential, and the need for more funds to fire-proof the wildland-urban interface is critical.

But it is also true that Californians and other Westerners must become a lot smarter about where they choose to live. If they decide to reside in fire zones, they need to learn how to safely inhabit those areas so as not to endanger the lives of those racing to their rescue.

In the immediate aftermath of the Station Fire, these cautionary insights have gone up in smoke. Now that fire has become so politicized, whenever and wherever sparks fly, a small army of firefighters will storm in and flame retardant will rain down.

Making this case in another form is University of Manitoba sociologist Mark Hudson. In *Fire Management in the American West: Forest Politics and the Rise of Megafires*, he challenges some of the uncritically accepted notions about the presence of massive blazes like the Station and Wallow Fires; he also upends other long-prevailing assumptions about the public's desire to compel fire managers to stamp out fire ever more vigorously from lands wild and domesticated.

Most compelling is Hudson's critique of the idea—so favored by environmentalists, journalists, and politicians—that the Forest Service is alone culpable for the devastating fires that have scorched so many acres since World War II.

Hudson does not doubt that the agency's robust fire-fighting infrastructure has contributed to the intensity of some recent conflagrations. He counters, however, that the usual extrapolation—that its suppressive actions have been the spark igniting a thousand flames—misses the larger point about who has had ultimate power over the nature of fire management in the United States.

"The project of eliminating fire from the woods and the 'blowback' of the increasing fire danger do not stem from the USFS as an isolated, highly autonomous body," Hudson asserts. "Rather, their roots are found in the Forest Service's relationships with other, more powerful elements of society—the timber industry in particular."

The blunt "refusal of capital and its representatives and allies in the US Congress to allow the Forest Service access to key tools that would have greatly increased its institutional capacity for management" did not diminish the agency's managerial responsibilities. It increased them. Ever since the Progressive Era, the agency has been charged with harvesting board feet of lumber from acre upon acre of green trees (unscorched, please!), and to do so without the authority to practice landscape-scale management—as if what happens on abutting private lands has no impact on public lands.

Here is how Hudson's argument plays out in Southern California. Southland residents, big-time developers, and their political minions demand that the Forest Service snuff out any and all fires on the Angeles, Los Padres, San Bernardino, and Cleveland National Forests. They would be infuriated, though, if the federal agency had the power to halt construction of homes, condos, and resorts in the foothills or mountains that the agency is charged with protecting.

We want to live where we want to live, we want to wring wealth from the unfettered development of the urban-wildland interface, and we expect—as owners and builders—that the Forest Service will subsidize our desires in its role as the national Fire Service. We want free will, just not the responsibility that comes with it.

Note, therefore, that Representative Schiff, his good constituency work aside, did not demand of those he represents that they acknowledge their complicity in the Station Fire's furious run. He did not acknowledge that the furor over the (mis)management of the Station Fire was an expression of our willful denial of the life-threatening implications of our decision to put down our roots inside the fire zone.

Until we can have an honest discussion about the formative role we play in generating the need for full-on fire suppression; until we accept that our eagerness to throw other people's bodies, and a ton of water and fire retardant at every puff of smoke comes, in Hudson's words, at a "high cost to the healthy functioning of many forest ecosystems"; until we concede that our demand that the Forest Service become a manager of "perpetual crisis," further crippling its capacity to act, we will never resolve these many dilemmas of our own making—and unmaking.

A Cautionary Tale

The fire started small. Someone deliberately ignited a pile of trash built up at the base of an oak tree in Griffith Park, a 4,300-acre municipal wildland draped across the Hollywood Hills. Within minutes, it had spread to the tinder-dry chaparral, running up what later was called Death Hill before whipping in and around Mineral Wells and Dam Canyons. By sundown, the Los Angeles County Fire Department had extinguished the forty-seven-acre blaze, and for the next couple of days its crews mopped up hot spots.

For all its seeming insignificance, October 3, 1933, was in fact historic, and deeply tragic. When supervisors of a large contingent of welfare project workers in the park spotted the first ominous curl of smoke, they threatened and cajoled their untrained men into attacking the fast-moving blaze with shovels, rakes, and their bare hands. Said one survivor: "It was just a lark to us. It didn't look dangerous then. We laughed about it and started down, to bat the fire out in a hurry."

Moments later, with a radical shift in the wind's direction and an escalation in its speed, the fire raced toward the hapless men. "You could tell the progress of the fire by the screams," one observer remembered. "The flames would catch a man and his screams would reach an awful pitch. Then there would be an awful silence. Then you would hear somebody scream and then it would be silent again. It was all over inside of seven minutes."

The official tally was that twenty-nine died, though some contemporary accounts put the toll as high as fifty-eight. Whatever their number, Griffith Park remains one of the nation's most deadly wildland fires.

Its horrific status resurfaced in the wake of yet another major loss of life as a result of the Yarnell Hill fire near Prescott, Arizona. On June 30, 2012, a bright, hot Sunday, an erratic, wind-driven wall of flame overran nineteen members of the Granite Mountain Hotshot crew.

There was nothing that one could say that would lessen the grief of their many loved ones, their network of friends and colleagues. Nothing could fill the void, an aching emptiness that will stretch across time.

Yet these painful memories may also be the catalyst for a major reconsideration of how we decide to fight fires in an era of population growth and climate change in the American West. Some of these recalibrations might emerge as a result of an intense investigation into the meteorological conditions, fire behavior, on-the-ground leadership, communications, and a host of other variables that existed on that fatal Sunday.

This analysis, Carrie Dennett, an Arizona State Forestry Division fire-prevention officer, told the *Arizona Republic*, "will be designed so we can learn from this and teach up-and-coming firefighters, if there are any lessons that can be learned."

Jack Ward Thomas is among those hoping Yarnell Hill will force the issue on whether, and under what conditions, to engage with runaway fires. "I have been having nightmares—again—over the loss of the hotshot crew in Arizona," the former Forest Service chief wrote me. "I was at Storm King in 1994 when the fourteen bodies were still in place. What I saw, heard, and felt still haunts my dreams. My God! Is it not time to face the realities—the worsening realities—and deal with the situation comprehensively?"

The pressing need for comprehensiveness begins with past behavior, for as Thomas implies, we have ignored similar warnings after other heart-rending traumas.

This pattern of forgetfulness began in 1910 with the Big Blowup, a series of separate fires in mountainous Idaho and Washington that were united by gale-force winds into a howling holocaust; it incinerated 3 million acres and killed seventy-eight firefighters. We have been dealing with the aftershocks of that disaster ever since.

The Forest Service, then in its infancy, decided that it must accelerate the training of its firefighters, adopt new tools on the ground and in the air, and ramp up its efforts to suppress any such blaze. By the 1930s it had announced the so-called 10 a.m. Rule, which called for all fires, regardless of context or condition, to be extinguished by the morning after they had been spotted. Although more honored in the breach, the promulgation inculcated an aggressive culture of firefighting and led to the swift adoption of innovative technologies to stamp out all subsequent outbursts.

The major proponent of this strategy, Ferdinand Silcox, then chief of the agency, had fought the 1910 fires in Montana and at the time had been skeptical of the ability of human resources to do the job in extreme situations: "It is absolutely impossible to put out such fires as are raging in the mountains now without the aid of rain," he told a reporter. "The entire northwest is as dry as tinder and the draft from the fires carries embers and burning branches miles away into the woods."

Twenty years later Silcox reached a different conclusion—given enough men and material, even monster conflagrations should be attacked at all costs.

That conviction was woven into the determination to take on the Mann Gulch Fire of 1949. Fifteen smokejumpers parachuted near a wind-whipped inferno in the mountains above Helena, Montana, where they joined a ranger who had hiked in to battle the rapidly moving blaze. Trapped near a ridgeline, thirteen died. In its post-fire investigation, the Forest Service exonerated the fire boss's decision to jump in the first place and his management decisions during the increasingly ferocious and unpredictable burn.

"I really think that the fire we saw when we flew over there was a typical smokejumper fire," one of the crew later confirmed. "And if they didn't jump on that fire they wouldn't have jumped on half the fires they jumped on that year. So I don't think it was a mistake to jump. After we got on the ground I think it was a freak of nature that caused the wind to do what it did and to pick those coals up and drop them in the canyon below us." Because smokejumping had been invented, the agency needed to use this tool notwithstanding any such "freak of nature."

Unfortunately, those freakish moments have piled up. Between 1949 and 2012, burnovers killed an estimated 221 of the 769 wildland firefighters who have died on the job.

The 1950s and '60s were especially harrowing on the California national forests. In 1953, fifteen died in a burnover in the Mendocino National Forest (NF); the next year, three more were lost in the Tahoe NF, and then in 1956 another eleven fell in the Cleveland NF. Ten years later, a dozen firefighters were killed in the Angeles NF, also the site of a 1968 incident in which four perished.

Following the 1994 fire season, in which fourteen firefighters were killed in the South Canyon Fire on Storm King Mountain near Glenwood Springs, Colorado, the Forest Service and other federal and state agencies embraced a more rigorous safety-first strategy, hoping to limit the number of fatalities.

The Yarnell tragedy suggested that we may not have fully absorbed this painful, century-long history.

The problem does not appear to be one of policy but of memory. We don't seem to know how to recall this deadly past, to keep it front and center, so as to understand why we need to abide by the rules and regulations already in place.

The public, moreover, must deliberately integrate these deaths into our ongoing education about fire's essential place in the landscape, whether grassland, chaparral, or alpine. They must also be a required discussion item before every zoning commission or city council vote to permit yet another subdivision in the wildland-urban interface. For make no mistake, we are undeniably complicit in this mounting toll—each fire season, and they are getting longer, we send firefighters out to do the work that might lead to their demise even as we have contributed to the increased frequency and intensity of the fires they battle on our behalf. They die where we live.

To ensure that their numbers do not grow, perhaps next time we'll remember what happened during the Big Blowup and in Griffith Park, at Mann Gulch, South Canyon, and now Yarnell Hill. Perhaps next time we won't forget what we have always known.

Burning News

After the 2013 Rim Fire blasted into Sierra Nevada granite and flickered out. After the last gallon of fire retardant rained down on the high-country blaze located deep in the Stanislaus National Forest. After the last engine, dozer, helicopter, jet, and drone pulled back from the charred land. After the last hose was drained, dried, and stored. After the last Pulaski was racked. After the last soot-stained firefighter retraced her steps to base camp, and then headed home. After all that, it was already (or maybe only nearly) too late to plan for a different fire future.

Our culture's relentless focus on the now has shaped the way the media covered (and we have anxiously followed) this particular fire and any conflagration dating back to the late nineteenth century. Journalism's daily mission, after all, is to keep us abreast of the news as it breaks, the very language of which emphasizes the need to mirror the moment.

Reflect on that as you flip through your local newspaper, watch your favorite newsreader, or scroll through relevant websites. Note how every story about a wildland fire contains a powerful one-word mantra: containment.

As you repeatedly enunciate it, absorbing its Cold War evocation of sealing off the "enemy," a series of worried questions are unleashed: Is the fire contained? How much is it contained? Why has more containment not been achieved? When, oh when will it be contained?

In the long run, these queries and the worry they convey are misdirected because they frame the discussion around the resources that are being rushed to the fire front—human, technological, and fiscal. One consequence is that media coverage is thus locked in on the loaded rhetoric of devastation. Hence the tallying each day of new acres scorched, homes incinerated, campgrounds burned, structures threatened, the number of people evacuated; and to what degree such grim ends have been averted, thanks to an expanding line of containment.

As the electronic and print media publish this data of damage and disarray, there is little room left for more sustained reflections of what this fire (or any other) means. The first step to securing that knowledge, the planet's best fire historian, Stephen J. Pyne, has repeatedly enjoined, is to complicate how we talk about fire.

Set aside the concept that fires inevitably, irreparably destroy forests and consider instead the idea that fire may have regenerative capacity. This simple switch of terms would compel us—writers and readers—to discover that there is a long history of high-intensity burns in the

Sierra Nevadas and that they have served, as the Rim Fire did as well, a critical ecological function.

By opening up dense forest cover, large fires enable some fire-adapted species to take advantage of the burn, just as happens in the Rockies, Wasatch, San Jacintos, and Sawtooths. Among those that will maximize their use of post–Rim Fire habitats, argues Chad Hanson of the Earth Island Institute, are the black-backed woodpecker and its food source, wood-boring beetles, along with such opportunistic browsers as deer and black bear.

Not all of fire's consequences are as obviously beneficial, at least not for those of us dependent on mountainous watersheds to sustain our thirsty downstream communities. Yet it turns out that in this context too, words, and the thoughts and actions they generate, matter.

Although some reports about the Rim Fire highlighted San Francisco's complete reliance on the Hetch Hetchy reservoir, located inside Yosemite National Park, these stories were freighted with dire anticipation—will airborne ash clog up the reservoir's century-old infrastructure, imperiling the City by the Bay's supply of potable water and electricity?

The immediate answer was no, which led the San Francisco Public Utilities Commission to predict that due "to the rocky, granite terrain and limited brush along the perimeter of the reservoir, there is little risk for direct impacts on the reservoir."

Whatever relief this instant response may have brought to thirsty San Franciscans, it may only be temporary and is certainly partial; it may not even be the right question. That is because at the time the more significant query, because it would have compelled analysts to think across a multiyear future, was what would happen when in the winter rain and snow swept down along the high-elevation watershed of the Tuolumne River that feeds into the threatened reservoir.

Given the bone-dry winters following the Rim Fire, the millions who partake of the crystal-clear water that backs up behind the O'Shaughnessy Dam, the linchpin to San Francisco's waterworks, did not wake up one morning to discover that storms had pounded the burned-over terrain, triggering debris flows that compromised the water quality within and the functioning of the Hetch Hetchy reservoir as spigot and generator.

Just because it did not happen does not mean that it cannot, as residents of Denver will confirm. In 2002, the Hayman Fire, at the time the most massive and most intense blaze in Colorado history, scorched 140,000 acres, much of them covering the upper reaches of the Mile High City's water supply. Ever since, the American Planning Association has reported, the tributaries of the Upper South Platte River have experienced an "increase in the number and severity of flooding events," which in turn has let loose "large amounts of sediment and debris threaten[ing] the vitality of watersheds and ecosystems."

These devastating postfire environmental consequences accelerated public and private collaborations to
restore affected riparian ecosystems. Grassroots groups
such as the Coalition for the Upper South Platte, which
coordinated an impressive 40,000 volunteer hours of
labor aimed at replanting denuded canyons and slopes,
have remained active in restoring the land. These groups
were the shock troops for two particular agencies, Denver
Water, the regional water purveyor, and the U.S. Forest Service, which manages the Pike National Forest, where the
arson-ignited fire erupted. In an important, collaborative
move, using federal funding through its Forest to Faucet
initiative, the Forest Service matched Denver Water's
$16.5 million grant to the agency, channeling $33 million
into cleanup and regeneration efforts on 38,000 acres of
high-risk lands. Rebuilding more fire-resilient and resistant forests was a win-win for the environment and the
downstream consumers of its life-giving waters.

Santa Fe, New Mexico, had been a model for the
Denver project. The city is heavily dependent on the Santa
Fe River for its water, a riparian system whose headwaters
drain the Sangre de Cristo Mountains to the east. When
it learned that the 2000 Cerro Grande Fire had badly
damaged Los Alamos, New Mexico's watershed, and cost
that city more than $17 million to repair what it had lost
in the conflagration, public officials in Santa Fe moved
quickly. Securing a one-time congressional earmark to pay
for the first phase of forest thinning along key portions of

the Santa Fe River watershed, the bulk of which lies in the eponymous national forest, they also won a small planning grant from the Forest Service to determine two things— how much the larger thinning project would cost (which they later calculated was $4.3 million over twenty years) and how they were going to pay for this necessary if pricey restoration. Borrowing a best practice that the Nature Conservancy had piloted in Ecuador, in which down-stream consumers paid for upstream vegetation manage-ment and watershed protection, the city polled ratepayers, who supported it by a whopping 82 percent.

Even Los Angeles, which has a long and controver-sial history of ignoring local water supplies in favor of imported water from the western slope of the Rockies and Sierra Nevada drainages, took notice of what occurred in Denver and Santa Fe. Shortly after the 2009 Station Fire, which damaged key portions of the Los Angeles and San Gabriel River watersheds, LA County and City, along with the Forest Service and the National Forest Foundation, raised funds to regenerate forest cover, river flow, and water quality.

It is striking, then, that San Francisco did not pick up on these broad hints and in advance work with local, state, and federal agencies to reduce the threat that a fire like the Rim could pose to its single-source water supply. But this would have required the city's Public Utility Commission and Division of Public Works to think proactively, for journalists there and elsewhere to offer more historically informed stories contextualizing wildland blazes across time and space, and for us collectively to build a more forward-thinking culture determined to resolve problems before they blow up in our faces.

Maybe that is a lot to ask, but surely it is preferable to taking passive comfort in headlines like the one splashed across the August 29, 2013, edition of the *Los Angeles Times*: "Rim Fire Containment Expected Sept. 10."

Hot Topic

Southern California burns. That is a given. It has over time, and will continue to do so.

What is not preordained is how we respond to the wildland flames that erupt on distant mountains or nearby foothills, scorching hundreds, even thousands of acres. Or, as is the case with the small, seventeen-acre brush fire on the Robert J. Bernard Field Station, an outdoor research lab owned by the Claremont Colleges, to a relatively undeveloped piece of property that is surrounded by residential neighborhoods and the community's many educational institutions.

And what we say, what we demand, what we conclude about these fiery events, large or little, says a great deal about our understanding of our place within this region's fire-adapted ecosystems.

That's why the particulars, the details matter. This two-alarm fire—dubbed the Foothill Fire—erupted quickly on the afternoon of September 11, 2013, and moved fast.

Its anthropogenic ignition, eyewitnesses noted, and LA County Fire investigators subsequently confirmed, occurred when a crew from Golden State Water Company employed a chop saw and torch while fixing an on-site, aboveground water pipe. The resulting shower of sparks kicked off the blaze (and even as flames swept north and east, these men continued to cut pipe on Foothill Boulevard, which delineates the field station's southern border, shooting more sparks into the air; I watched them bounce off nearby eucalyptus). One way of interpreting this fire's significance, then, is framed around human error—incautious actions, unsafe behavior were responsible for the blaze. End of story.

There is, however, another framework by which to read this event: Even though its point of origin may not have been "natural," the Foothill Fire has had profound implications for the colleges' field station and the many faculty and students who study its unique biota. Enter history: the 85-acre site constitutes part of the 250-acre parcel that philanthropist Ellen Browning Scripps purchased in the 1920s to launch Scripps College (other colleges and institutes now also occupy portions of her formative gift of the land). A series of unsuccessful plans for the remaining acreage, combined with local scientists making use of the undeveloped terrain for informal teaching and research, turned the land into an informal outdoor laboratory. That process became more formalized in the mid-1970s, after another attempt to sell the property led a longtime supporter of the colleges to donate funds to purchase it from the Scripps Trust and name it after Bernard, another committed booster of the consortium of colleges. His was an apt choice, for he perfectly understood the field station's educational benefit: "A tour of the property readily convinces visitors of the importance of keeping such a beautiful expanse of land, shrubs, and trees for scientific purposes."

Its import is readily explained by the fact that ever since then researchers at the field station—faculty with whom I studied and those with whom I now teach—have particularly concentrated on exploring the geology, soils, and biology of those patches of rare coastal sage scrub ecosystem that the site encompasses. Because most of this landscape, once the dominant plant community in the Southland, has been bulldozed away for development, what remains in the Bernard Field Station is particularly invaluable. And it was made even more so when some of it went up in smoke during the Foothill Fire, offering an unparalleled opportunity for teachers and students to analyze how this imperiled plant community regenerates—in what manner, how quickly, and to what degree.

One of the factors that has shaped this research emerged even as my colleagues and I watched the helicopters and Super Scooper aircraft fly sortie after sortie over the inferno, as we witnessed the churning thick dark smoke turn white with every water drop, as we (foolishly) inhaled the acrid air: everyone was calculating which plots across the street were ablaze, speculating how soon they might be allowed back on the ground to assess the damage and begin to reformulate their experimental sites to capture postfire alterations and opportunisms.

The speed with which the flames moved also caught our eye. Paul Faulstich, a cultural ecologist on the faculty at Pitzer College who regularly teaches classes incorporating the Field Station's ecological riches, observed: "It was interesting to see how the fire moved through the coastal sage scrub in the center of the Field Station at a moderate pace, but when it hit the nonnative grasses in the eastern portion it accelerated and ravaged the land."

He and others pointed out that the indigenous plants were burning differently, too: "If you stand at the fence and look in you can see this quite readily," said Faulstich, who was on the scene just before the first fire engines screamed up. "The sage scrub environment has stems and branches of native plants remaining, while the nonnative grassland area is essentially demolished."

His insight is confirmed by ongoing research by the Chaparral Institute into the escalating dangers that invasive grasses pose to regional biodiversity and to the firefighters called on to snuff out hazardous, grass-fueled conflagrations such as the 2006 Esperanza Fire in Riverside County, during which five firefighters lost their lives. That is why Richard Halsey, the institute's director, has argued in support of protecting the original shrublands of Southern California: "If we really want to save lives, safeguard property and protect the environment, we need to adapt to the environment instead of making the environment adapt to us."

The Foothill Fire will help determine what that adaptive process might look like. My colleagues and their students are tracking the rates of individual plant die-offs, when and where reseeding occurs, and whether fire-scarred shrubs, bushes, and trees are rejuvenating. They are also assessing the capacity of insects, birds, coyotes, and rodents to respond to the loss of food and shelter (and its revival). Some are probing the complicated but fascinating process known as commensalism, the association that can exist between two organisms wherein one benefits and the other neither gains nor loses—much like the so-called fire beetle, which makes a beeline to torched terrain, gathering on still-smoldering branches to mate and subsequently lay its eggs. Claremont students are having a field day on this postfire terrain, a living lab that exemplifies their dynamic engagement with this evolving landscape and the educational mission that the field station's namesake first identified.

These fertile prospects even seemed to have received a kind of prospective benediction when the Super Scooper airplanes angled low over the fire, then soared up, dropping their wet payloads. As the water cascaded down, one rainbow after another bloomed forth, a band of primary colors arching across the charcoal-gray sky.

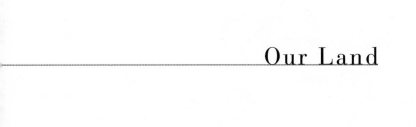

Our Land

Does the Past Have Standing?

The Antiquities Act has itself become old, at least by American standards. Congress enacted the legislation, one of the nation's most significant environmental initiatives, in 1906. What makes the act (16 USC 431-433) so profound is that it grants the president discretionary power to set aside portions of our public lands as national monuments so as to protect those "historic landmarks, historic and prehistoric structures, and other objects of historic or scientific interest that are situated upon the lands owned or controlled by the Government of the United States."

Its chief proponents in the late nineteenth century were historians, scientists, and archaeologists infuriated by the routine pillaging of ancient ruins across the Southwest, the rampant desecration of sacred sites. These professionals found sympathetic politicians, most notably Representative John Lacey (R-Iowa), who six years earlier was instrumental in the passage of the first federal law prohibiting the transportation, possession, or sale of illegally taken wildlife, plants, and fish. Naturally, he became the floor manager of the Antiquities Act, shepherding it through countless hearings, committee meetings, and votes. But the person most closely associated with it as a living document, as a political reality, is the president whose signature turned it into law: Theodore Roosevelt.

The Antiquities Act is the perfect Roosevelt piece of legislation: it authorized the executive branch to manage the public lands more carefully and regulate the uses to which they are put. It heightened Americans' awareness of the need for greater sensitivity to and more efficient stewardship of the nation's cultural landmarks and environmental resources, all matters of great concern to this devoted conservationist and prolific historian of the West. And it enhanced the clout of the presidency, another subject close to Roosevelt's heart.

He knew exactly what to do with this congressionally sanctioned authority, too. During the last six months of 1906, Roosevelt announced the establishment of four national monuments, among them Devils Tower in Wyoming; El Morro in New Mexico; and two in Arizona, Montezuma Castle and Petrified Forest.

Roosevelt was just getting warmed up. In 1907, he added another five national monuments; the next year he signed off on an additional eight, including Muir Woods and the Grand Canyon (later rededicated as a national park). Roosevelt's run concluded in March 1909, when two days before he left the White House, he brought Washington's Mount Olympus into the fold. In a little more than two years, he had designated eighteen national monuments, setting a very high bar for his successors (none of whom has cleared it).

TR's conservation commitments today rankle those who populate his former political home, the Republican Party. Its current members happily forget that the Antiquities Act was a GOP initiative signed by one of its most formidable presidents. They are delighted not to recall that the founding chief of the Forest Service, Gifford Pinchot, like Stephen Mather, the founding director of the National Park Service—the two agencies then responsible for protecting national monuments (the Bureau of Land Management did not yet exist)—were also staunch Republicans. They have no memory that elephants once were a deep green.

How did these political pachyderms change their colors? Thanks to the two presidents Roosevelt. Theodore bolted from the party in the run-up to the 1912 election, lashing out at its fat-cat cronyism and launching the Bull Moose ticket, a move that torpedoed William Howard Taft's reelection bid. With no home inside the GOP, progressives began to shift to the Democratic column, especially with the emergence of Franklin D. Roosevelt as that party's 1932 standard-bearer.

Like his cousin, FDR pursued an active conservation agenda, aided by a Great Depression that allowed him to use public funds to purchase abandoned farms and ranches for new national forests and grasslands. His agenda was expanded further through the creation of the

Civilian Conservation Corps and other initiatives that put thousands of men and women to work planting cutover, grazed, and eroded terrain, repairing the land and rehabilitating the people.

Along the way Roosevelt also enlarged Glacier Bay National Monument by 900,000 acres; added eleven new sites, including the first desert parks, Death Valley and Joshua Tree; and brought into the fold the Channel Islands off the Southern California coast. None was as controversial as the last, however: Wyoming's Jackson Hole, 210,000 acres that the Rockefeller family donated to the federal government. Its designation generated a furious counterattack. Angered that the president had invoked the Antiquities Act only after Congress had refused to enlarge Grand Teton, legislators enacted a measure aimed at abolishing the new national monument. FDR vetoed it. As a compromise, after court challenges failed to decertify the president's actions, Congress finally folded the Jackson Hole acreage into the adjacent Grand Teton National Park. But its enabling legislation contained a provision prohibiting any future use of the Antiquities Act in Wyoming, which Roosevelt accepted.

This battle royal neatly illustrates the striking transition that had occurred in terms of which party dominated national conservation policy. Democrats had captured what Republicans once controlled—the political conviction that conservation was a social necessity, that the federal government should advance environmental protections, and that the president was the conservationist-in-chief.

Having conceded this high ground, the GOP were left to allege that whenever the chief executive makes use of the Antiquities Act he has been undercutting congressional prerogatives and states' rights. Republicans made extensive use of this one-time Democratic rhetoric to hammer Jimmy Carter after his December 1, 1978, hypersigning national monument ceremony, during which he created fifteen new national monuments in Alaska. They did so again in 1996 to lambaste Bill Clinton after he put his signature on the act establishing Utah's Grand Staircase–Escalante National Monument.

The Republican Party made free use of this rhetoric, too, after it snagged control of the U.S. House of Representatives in the 2010 by-elections. The chair and subcommittee chairs of the Natural Resources Committee used their positions to launch attacks on such indispensable environmental legislation as the Wilderness Act (1964), the National Environmental Policy Act (1969), and the Endangered Species Act (1973). But they and their supporters had a special disdain for the Antiquities Act. In the spring and summer of 2012, for example, they mounted a sustained effort to gut John Lacey's legislation. Indeed, as an early, anti-106th birthday present, that April the GOP and some of its conservative Democratic allies pushed through Congress the so-called Sportsmen's Heritage Act of 2012.

HR 4089 attempted to break open the Wilderness Act's court-tested primacy in defining land-management practices within officially designated wildlands and would have forced the U.S. Forest Service, the Fish and Wildlife Service, and the Bureau of Land Management to allow motorized transportation in wilderness, and energy development, among other noncompatible uses. It included provisions that allowed hunters to use lead ammunition on the U.S. public lands, directly circumventing EPA regulations that prohibited this form of toxic ammunition. Early versions of the bill, which did not make it into the final in 2012, also contained anti–Antiquities Act language that would have compelled the chief executive to secure approval from the relevant *state* legislatures (and governors) before altering the designated status of *federal* public land. In short, it would have taken away the president's authority to denote national monuments.

Although this bill passed the House, it failed in the Democratic-controlled Senate, as did a successor piece of legislation, HR 3590, dubbed "Sportsmen's Heritage and Recreational Enhancement Act of 2014." One year later, after the Republican by-election sweep netted the GOP majority power in both houses of the U.S. Congress, a new version of the Sportsmen's Act reappeared, testifying to the Republican Party's persistent dislike of the Antiquities Act, the Wilderness Act, and a host of related environmental regulations governing the use of the national grasslands, forests, and refuges.

Not all western voters are enamored of such blunt assaults on the Antiquities Act. No sooner had the Sportsmen's Heritage Act of 2012 surfaced than local groups and a bipartisan array of political representatives in the states of Colorado, Washington, and Idaho began demanding that the president use his Antiquities Act authority to announce the creation respectively of the proposed Chimney Rock, Greater Canyonlands, and San Juan Islands National Monuments. In Los Angeles, there was concerted pressure to denote the San Gabriel Mountains National Monument within the Angeles National Forest, and on the north coast of the Golden State proponents urged the expansion of the California Coastal National Monument.

In each instance, the proponents decried the actions of Representatives Doc Hastings (R-WA) and Rob Bishop (R-UT)—then Natural Resources chair and subchair, respectively—for bottling up their representatives' efforts to secure legislative approval from the Natural Resources Committee. "Because of the difficulties in getting any legislation through the current Congress," argued Dan Rudolph, executive director of the San Juan (CO) Citizens Alliance, in the *Durango Herald*, "the push for national monument status has now shifted to asking President Barack Obama to designate the site through the Antiquities Act. . . . Chimney Rock, with its important historical and cultural significance, is a perfect example of what the act was intended to protect."

As frustrated, and with greater reason, are Navaho, Zuni, Ute, and Hopi tribal members who have, in collaboration with the Bureau of Land Management, Forest Service, and Park Service, devised a unique land-management strategy for nearly 2 million acres in Utah—a plan that would serve as a template for incorporating tribal entities as full partners in managing, say, Gila National Forest, Grand Canyon National Park, and Malheur National Wildlife Refuge. It is important in this regard that since 2010 the Navaho, Zuni, Hopi, and Ute have negotiated with an array of local communities, special interests, and political representatives to secure consensus in support of Bear Ears National Monument, which would secure for the tribes increased authority over its protection and preservation, including the use of traditional knowledge and tribal spirituality to frame the site's management. It would also ensure greater access to sacred sites, from which they have been excluded in the past. As Malcolm Lehi, a member of the Ute people, told former interior secretary Bruce Babbitt, a staunch supporter of the project: "We can still hear the songs and prayers of our ancestors on every mesa and in every canyon."

Representative Rob Bishop has no interest in those voices or the collaborative processes that have produced this imaginative monument initiative. In January 2016, after years of stalling, he offered legislation to the Republican-dominated House subcommittee he chaired that instead encouraged intensified resource extraction and road development on the lands in question; to further obliterate the national monument's prospects, he inserted what Babbitt decried in the *Los Angeles Times* as a "'gag rule' so unusual that it is without precedent in land-management legislation. It stipulates that federal agencies cannot consider or take into account any tribal recommendation that has not been endorsed in advance by either the state of Utah or a local county commission."

It is an open question whether the president will wield his Antiquities Act authorities in the final year of his second term, but by its rights Bear Ears would warrant it. So would the expansion of Roosevelt Historic National Park. For years Theodore Roosevelt IV and Tweed Roosevelt, two of TR's great-grandsons, have fought to expand the Roosevelt National Historic Park, situated in the rough Badlands of western North Dakota. Of special interest is acreage surrounding Elkhorn Ranch, to which the future president retreated in 1884 after the near-simultaneous deaths of his beloved wife and mother. Its solitude, which brought Roosevelt such solace, remains threatened by proposed gravel-pit operations and oil-and-gas drilling nearby, access to which would be facilitated by the construction of a new bridge across the Little Missouri River.

What better way to maintain this landscape's raw power and its historic claim on our cultural imagination, the cousins and their allies have long argued, than for President Obama to offer Antiquities Act protection to the landed legacy of our most important environmental president? In 2014, during yet another congressional attempt to undercut the Antiquities Act, TR IV denounced the legislation as "a misguided bill that will turn America's cultural and natural legacy upside down—taking us from a country that seeks protection for its iconic scenery and historical heritage to one that creates obstacles to preserving these incredible places." His was a call for a return to first principles, a critical line of defense for the Antiquities Act.

Malheur Occupied

The Malheur National Wildlife Refuge, a 187,757-acre haven for greater sandhill cranes and other native and migratory birds in eastern Oregon, is usually a pretty peaceful place. But its calm was shattered on January 2, 2016, when Ammon Bundy and a group of armed men broke into and occupied a number of federal buildings on the refuge, vowing to fight to the death should the government try to arrest them. Their insurrectionary goal, simply put, is to destroy the national system of public lands—our forests, parks, and refuges—that was developed in the late nineteenth century to conserve these special landscapes and the critical natural resources they contain for all Americans.

"The best possible outcome," trumpeted Bundy, son of the Cliven Bundy who began an armed standoff with law enforcement in Nevada in April 2014 over his continued failure to pay $1 million in fees for grazing on public lands, is that "ranchers that have been kicked out of the area . . . will come back and reclaim their land, and the wildlife refuge will be shut down forever and the federal government will relinquish such control." Theirs was not a rebellion, Bundy declared. "What we're doing is in accordance with the Constitution, which is the supreme law of the land."

He could not be more wrong. To understand why requires a basic understanding of the region's complex and troubling history and the legal authority under which the federal land-management agencies operate.

The Paiute, after all, have first claim to this now-disputed land, a point they asserted in their blunt rejection of the Bundy-led occupation of the refuge. "Don't tell me any of these ranchers came across the Bering Strait," Charlotte Rodrique, the tribe's chairwoman, told the *New York Times*. "We were here first." For millennia, and thus long before settler-colonists arrived in the region, the Paiute hunted, fished, and gathered in this fertile, albeit arid, terrain. Their remarkable ecological adaptability, observes historian Nancy Langston in *Where the Land and Water Meet* (2003), the definitive study of the Malheur Basin, helped the colonists rationalize their post–Civil War eviction: "Whites looked at the Paiutes and believed they saw a people who had no fixed habitation, no material culture, no cultivation, no livestock, no homes, and no real claim to humanness."

Battered into submission, crowded into a reservation, and prohibited from acting on their treaty rights to hunt and fish off-reservation, in the late 1870s the Paiute fought back, but the U.S. Army crushed their brief uprising, and the consequences were grim: their local reservation was shut down and its lands returned to the public domain; shackled and under armed guard, the indigenous people were forced-marched through the snow 350 miles to the Yakama reservation in southeastern Washington State. Although in time they would return to southeastern Oregon to land granted them in and around the Malheur refuge, the Paiute, who for thirteen centuries had inhabited this basin, know full well the meaning of the French word applied to it—misfortune, adversity.

The land suffered, too. It is no coincidence that dispossessing the Paiute allowed large livestock operations to take over, resulting in the rapid deterioration of the grasslands in the upper reaches of the Silvies and Blitzen Rivers, which flow into Malheur Lake. Further diminishing the lake's capacity to sustain migratory and local bird populations were the irrigation and drainage projects that the Bureau of Reclamation, founded in 1902 to manage water to boost economic development in the arid West, built upstream.

Add to this despoliation the reckless hunt for bird plumage: late nineteenth-century fashionistas coveted the white heron's graceful feathers to adorn their hats. With gold rush–like avarice, local hunters blazed away, and within a few years the Malheur heron population was decimated.

It was their extirpation—not the brutal mistreatment of the Paiutes—that caught the attention of the Oregon Audubon Society. Its activists pleaded with President

Theodore Roosevelt, a former rancher and Rough Rider, to protect those lands still in federal ownership. On August 18, 1908, he complied, signing an executive order establishing the 81,786-acre Malheur Lake Refuge, which also encompassed nearby Haney and Mud Lakes, "as a preserve and breeding ground for native birds." Since then, the refuge has expanded by 100,000 acres. In 1935, the Swift Meatpacking Corporation sold 65,000 acres to the federal government, funding for which came from Duck Stamp sales and New Deal monies; over the years, willing sellers added to the refuge's expanse. Ammon Bundy's protestations to the contrary, no ranchers were ever evicted from the refuge.

Just as disingenuous is Bundy's militant bluster about restoring the Constitution by tossing the federal government off the Malheur and other public lands because these acres belong to settler descendants. They do not and never have. Consider that the Oregon Statehood Act of 1859 explicitly conceded that the federal government controlled whatever public lands were not granted to the state at the time of statehood (another key indicator of that concession—Oregon could not tax federal property). As outsiders, the Bundys and their ilk might plead ignorance of this particular legislation and its details. But they know that their home state of Nevada contains similar language in its constitution, for their father's many critics—including the Silver State's attorney general—were quick to publicize the relevant text: "That the people inhabiting said territory [Nevada] do agree and declare that they forever disclaim all right and title to the unappropriated public lands lying within said territory, and that the same shall be and remain at the sole and entire disposition of the United States."

The Bundys' argument also gets its comeuppance in a pair of landmark Supreme Court decisions in 1911. In *Light v. United States* (220 U.S. 523) and *United States v. Grimaud* (220 U.S. 506), the court asserted that federal ownership of the public lands was indisputable and that Congress through a series of legislative acts had granted the executive branch—and by extension the federal land-management agencies—administrative authority to manage these acres in accordance with the relevant rules and regulations.

These cases emerged out of the first Sagebrush Rebellion of the early twentieth century. Western livestock, mineral, and timber interests had exploded in anger at the redesignation of portions of the public domain into the national forests and the regulations that the newly created U.S. Forest Service enacted on grazing, mining, and logging. What changed was that ranchers, miners, and loggers were required to pay a small fee to access the relevant resources that once they had simply harvested for free.

As these special interests and their political minions lashed out, harassing rangers and threatening to rebel against the nation-state, they sought test cases to undercut the federal agency's regulatory authority; the Forest Service also had its day in court in hopes of establishing precedent for its managerial actions. They found them when Colorado cattleman Fred Light and California shepherd Pierre Grimaud were caught illegally grazing their herds on national forest land. The Colorado legislature even paid all of Light's legal expenses in hopes of proving its point that states, not the federal government, had sovereignty over the public lands within their borders. In May 1911, a highly conservative Supreme Court disagreed, ruling unanimously in the Forest Service's favor.

This precedent should have put an end to such challenges, but subsequent generations of would-be Sagebrushers have adopted the same hostile antifederal rhetoric and often-violent tactics. There were outbreaks in the 1920s, '40s, and '50s. During the Reagan and Bush administrations, fueled by vitriolic talk-show disdain for Washington, Nevada county commissioners crashed bulldozers through Forest Service fences to claim "ownership." Elsewhere, ranger offices were firebombed and agency equipment vandalized. More recently, in 2010 the Utah legislature asserted that it would use eminent domain to take over national monuments, grasslands, and forests. Four years later, Nevada rancher Cliven Bundy declared federal sovereignty null and void, refused to pay his grassland-leasing fees, and took up arms to face down the feds. His son's three-week-long occupation of the Malheur National Wildlife Refuge—which came to a violent end on

January 26, 2015—is but the latest in a long line of such confrontations.

Yet none of these persistent attacks has succeeded in dismantling the federal land-management agencies or the Supreme Court precedents that sanction their actions, a critical lesson from this contested past that Ammon Bundy and his co-conspirators so willfully ignored.

Condor Haven

The news was as bright as the day. It came in the form of a January 2013 email that arrived as we sped through the sun-drenched Salinas Valley, flicking past tractors tilling the fertile soil, work crews laying down irrigation pipes, and fields bearing winter crops of kale, red cabbage, and, one sign promised, "Romaine Lettuce: Coming Soon!" That exclamation mark was doubled as I scrolled through the much-anticipated announcement that President Obama had signed legislation turning Pinnacles National Monument into the nation's fifty-ninth national park. I looked up from the screen and saw the new park's signature landform, North Chalone Peak, filling the windshield; it and the rest of the Galiban Mountains dazzled in the crisp blue sky.

For all Pinnacles' striking beauty, for all its geological significance (its heights comprise the remnants of an ancient volcano), cultural resonance (the Ohlone people and others made good use of its upcountry woodlands and riparian habitats), and ecological richness (California condors have been successfully reintroduced here), none of these values by themselves were responsible for the initial creation of the national monument in 1908. None were critical to its redesignation as a national park. Both moments required a very human force: politics.

As with so many other origin stories about the national forests, monuments, and parks in the United States, President Theodore Roosevelt was present at the creation of Pinnacles National Monument. Indeed, it is a rare example of a site that has enjoyed protection under three different forms of federal management. Its initial 14,108 acres were set aside as the Pinnacles Forest Reserve in 1906, one year after the U.S. Forest Service had been created; in 1907, all forest reserves became known as national forests, a subtle shift in name that the agency's first chief, Gifford Pinchot, believed reflected their purposeful utility to all the American people.

There would be precious little logging in this particular forest, however. Its real value—as conservationists on the national level, like Roosevelt and Pinchot, and on the local, like Schuyler Hain, a homesteader and the landscape's most persistent booster, recognized—lay in a different kind of commodity: what we now call ecotourism.

Hain, for one, was convinced that the craggy terrain, and the numerous caves and native artifacts that he and others had located there, would draw curious travelers eager to know more about the young nation's distant past. He likened its entrance to "the doorway to the Garden of the Gods, but on a grander scale. Here the cliffs of many-colored rock rise hundreds of feet in sharply defined terraces, or great domes or pinnacles. Beyond, and scattered over an area of some six square miles is a mass of conglomerate rocks wonderful in extent and in fantastic variety of form and coloring."

As much to defend the Pinnacles' natural beauty and archeological resources as to promote his guide business, Hain advocated for a more consistent and rigorous protection of the parkland, a theme he pressed through a lantern slideshow that he toured through the region and in articles written for statewide publications.

The enterprising Hain also worked through connections at Stanford University to reach out to the local congressional representative and national figures such as forester Pinchot. University president David Starr Jordan was a crucial go-between, assuring Pinchot that the site was not only home to rare species that should be saved but also offered abundant recreational opportunities for an urbanizing Bay Area and contained a geological record unusual enough to warrant scientific investigation under controlled conditions. Apparently Pinchot then asked that the relevant acreage be "withdrawn from entry"—a technical term that meant that no grazing, logging, or mining claims could be filed on this portion of public land.

But it took Roosevelt's signature to make the national forest a national monument. With the 1906 passage of the Antiquities Act, which granted the chief executive the power to create such monuments on federal property to protect their indigenous artifacts and other special features, Roosevelt had a tool of considerable power, and he wielded it readily. Over the next four years, he created eighteen national monuments, from Devils Tower in Wyoming to Mount Olympus in what is now Olympic National Park in Washington State. During one week in January 1908 alone, TR proclaimed three new sites: Muir Woods in Marin County, the Grand Canyon, and Pinnacles.

The latter's proclamation stressed that because its "natural formations, known as the Pinnacles Rocks, with a series of caves underlying them . . . are of scientific value," their significance would now forever be reserved. It contained a key caution, too: "Warning is given to all unauthorized persons not to appropriate, injure, or destroy any feature of this National Monument or to locate or settle upon any of the lands reserved by this proclamation." By this act, Pinnacles was integrated into the nation's growing inventory of special places, a political landscape that defined how people could approach and appreciate its significance. Schuyler Hain must have been ecstatic.

Imagine his joy today, now that Pinnacles has become a national park. Strikingly, he would have little trouble recognizing the rhetorical devices embedded in the Department of the Interior's press release about the transition, for the language of preservation has changed little in the intervening years. "This ancient and awe-inspiring volcanic field with its massive monoliths, spires, cave passages and canyons is a place that restores our souls and energizes our bodies with its beauty and abundant opportunities for outdoor recreation,"

Interior Secretary Ken Salazar declared. Although Hain surely would have been stunned by the economic impact that recreation brings to the monument/park—in 2012 it welcomed nearly 350,000 visitors, who spent an estimated $4.8 million locally—the fact that this recreation has proved such an effective economic generator for the Salinas and San Benito Valleys was consistent with his original claims.

The political process that brought about the name change would also dovetail with his experience a century ago. As Hain rallied his friends and neighbors, he also had to reach out across the region to secure media attention, congressional interest, and executive branch action. Tapping into local, regional, and federal networks was essential to the success of his project.

It remains just as critical. Representative Sam Farr (D-Carmel), who had been pushing for this legislative change since the early 2000s and had enjoyed the support of such powerful Democrats as Senators Diane Feinstein and Barbara Boxer, did not gain serious traction until he built up a bipartisan coalition that included local chambers of commerce and environmental organizations; secured a Republican cosponsor, Representative Jeff Denham (R-Atwater); and agreed to drop plans to expand the monument's wilderness area by 3,000 acres. In a polarized Washington, the only way to secure even such a simple name change is to reach across the aisle.

This political context frames as well the stalled status of the proposed Greater Canyonlands National

Monument in southern Utah, a landscape that writer Stephen Trimble describes as a "magical rejuvenating" environment. Site of some of the richest archaeological records of native peoples anywhere, replete with ancient granaries, cliff dwellings, and rock art, its forests, grass-lands, rivers, and geological formations, according to the Southern Utah Wilderness Alliance, also shelter "at least two dozen endangered or sensitive species as well as an unusually large number of species found nowhere else in the world."

Little wonder that in the mid-1990s, after an extensive tour of the Red Rock region, a fact-finding group of prominent biologists, ecologists, and zoologists strongly urged the Bureau of Land Management to designate the site as part of the National Wilderness Preservation System, to safeguard and preserve "Utah's unique biological heritage." Efforts to secure that legacy have been as consistent as the opposition that they have annually generated. In 1989, Representative Wayne Owens filed the first of a long line of bills seeking wilderness protection for the area; he was a rare breed, a liberal Democrat in the thoroughly GOP-dominated state of Utah, and that surely accounts for why he found little support among his colleagues. When in 1992 he gave up his seat to run unsuccessfully for the U.S. Senate, his friend Representative Maurice Hinchey of New York carried on, filing one bill after another in coordination with Senator Dick Durbin (D-IL). Note that none of these later initiatives originated within the Utah delegation, and none will get to a vote until the state congressional delegation decides to support such legislation.

This roadblock is why the indefatigable Southern Utah Wilderness Alliance (SUWA) has urged President Obama to play Theodore Roosevelt, using the authority vested in the Oval Office through the Antiquities Act to declare a Greater Canyonlands National Monument. But it was another president's use of this executive power finesse that partly accounts for Utah Republicans' unwavering resistance to the establishment of another wilderness area in the Beehive State.

In September 1996, in the final weeks of a tense presidential campaign, incumbent Bill Clinton went to the Grand Canyon in Arizona—and, on its south rim, signed into law the Grand Staircase–Escalante National Monument, a vast tract of nearly 1.9 million acres in southern Utah. Across the border, a political furor erupted that has never really died down. Clinton's dramatic gesture, for all the environmental benefits it produced, made it exceedingly difficult for a subsequent chief executive to act as unilaterally.

SUWA activists might take solace in the long view. After all, Schuyler Hain and other early promoters of Pinnacles had hoped to secure national park status for the iconic Central California landscape; they and their successors had to plug away for more than a century before they achieved their original goal. Let's hope Greater Canyonlands reaches that promised land sooner than that.

Remember the Timbisha

It is not every day that you get panhandled by a coyote. At high noon. In Death Valley National Park.

Driving south from Badwater, on our way to the small town of Shoshone, just outside the park's southern entrance, we topped a rise and spotted a small mammal padding toward us down the middle of the black-topped highway. At first, because of its diminutive size, we took it for the endemic kit fox. But that made no sense, given that the sun was blazing away and the fox is a nocturnal prowler. It seemed just as odd that it might be a coyote, given that those we almost daily spot in our hometown are bigger, rangier, and tougher-looking, and they never, ever sidle up to cars or people. By contrast, this individual, and the more skittish one lurking off to the side of the road, seemed not just unfazed but utterly acclimated to our automotive presence. So much so that when we braked, the coyote swung off the road, trotted over to the passenger side window, tilted its head to the right, and stared. "It's begging," my wife exclaimed. Who knew that in one of the wildest spots on the planet, some of these superb scavengers have figured out how to hit up tourists for a tasty handout.

That in more significant ways humans have transformed the behavior of those living within the park's ecosystems is not all that surprising. After all, the creation
of what is now a 3.4-million-acre national park in Death
Valley, which followed a half century of mineral exploitation and town building in the remote site in the desert of
southeastern California, has been part of a larger process
by which this landscape has been altered.

As changed has been our appreciation of this spare,
dry, low, and oh-so-hot terrain. It wasn't that long ago that
most Euro-Americans thought the harsh Mojave Desert
contained nothing worth protecting. For most, it was
but a vast wasteland, a place of threat (its name is not a
misnomer), a landscape to be hurried through; after their
two-month ordeal trying to work their way through the
120-mile-long valley, a group of lost emigrants described
their 1849 experience as one haunted by "hunger and thirst
and an awful silence." It is hard to find anyone back in the
day who thought this arid terrain should be preserved for
its own sake.

Except, that is, its original inhabitants. The Shoshone people, especially those known as the Timbisha,
who for millennia have roamed the place we now call
Death Valley, had brilliantly adapted to the oft-harsh life
within its basins, foothills, and mountains. Nothing about
this seemingly forbidding landscape was for them a wasteland or wilderness. It was (and remains) simply home, a
source of food and shelter, art and culture, a spirit world

into which their communal life has been deeply interwoven. One who captured this integration is Mary Austin, who lived on the eastern slope of the Sierra and whose *The Land of Little Rain* (1903) contains some of the most sensitive and sympathetic portrayals of the indigenous people inhabiting "the free air and free spaces of Shoshone Land."

This tight weave between people and place was rent by the nineteenth-century arrival of explorers, treaty makers, cartographers, and the U.S. Army, as well as legions of miners, land speculators, railroad crews, cross-country migrants, and some settlers. Their grasping presence, resource extraction, and hegemonic power slowly unraveled the capacity of the Timbisha to maintain their historic relationship to the desert.

No less disruptive in this regard was the arrival of the National Park Service, which secured control over Death Valley in 1933 when President Hoover declared it a national monument. His proclamation set aside almost 2 million acres "for the preservation of the unusual features of scenic, scientific, and educational interest," warned against anyone vandalizing, injuring, or removing "any feature of this monument," and prohibited people from locating or settling inside its boundaries. It is revelatory that when John R. White, the park's first superintendent, arrived on the site, he was startled to discover that the Timbisha existed at all, let alone that they lived within what had just been designated a national monument. Some of his successors would prove more generous than others, but on the whole the National Park Service had little interest in sharing Death Valley with them.

Effectively exiled, the Timbisha would not regain a legally recognized homeland inside park boundaries until the 1994 California Desert Protection Act added a million acres to Death Valley and compelled the National Park Service to cede some land to them, a toehold in what had been their vast home ground.

In the interim, and consistent with the federal agency's belief that wilderness is the antithesis of civilization—a place apart where people can visit but not live—park administrators also have fought for the past eighty years to restrict mining and other nonrecreational activities inside Death Valley. Although not entirely successful in this quest, the Mining in the Parks Act of 1976 helped close many shafts and pits and block the development of new ones.

Corralling the burgeoning burro population, killing off invasive plants and trees, and stabilizing the endangered pupfish, an ice age relict living within Salt Creek's brackish waters, have critically defined the Park Service's managerial efforts, to restore as best as possible its ecological integrity, a more pristine character.

Stewarding the wild also comes with an aesthetic judgment. Although she was not the first to voice this perspective, feminist Edna Brush Perkins, a Philadelphian who visited the valley in the early 1920s, wrote glowingly of what she encountered. "We knew that the valley was sterile and dead, yet we saw it covered with a mantle of such strange beauty that we felt it was the noblest thing we had ever imagined." Since then, and in growing numbers, other tourists have responding to the stark, jagged, and windswept land with equal measures of awe and fear. And many of these have wanted to test themselves against its harsh conditions. Given this hunger to rough it, and the impact that this demand has been having on the iconic landforms that bring so many to the park, the agency has established tighter regulations governing the size of camping groups, the extent of commercial and noncommercial use of its rugged features, and the location and timing of specialized recreational activities like sandboarding, canyoneering, and caving. To institute greater managerial control over these and other uses, in 2012 the agency released a Wilderness and Backcountry Stewardship Plan whose purpose has been to make this wild land a little more wild.

Surely it is a bit paradoxical, however understandable, that human management of wilderness is essential to preserve it as wilderness. Or, that this conceit can so easily be complicated by the presence of a pack of supplicating coyotes.

Mojave Mirage

Everything has changed. Driving into the Mojave Desert after an absence of forty years, my wife and I were struck by the density of the human presence. It is not that we expected *nothing* to have happened in the intervening decades, but we were unprepared for the extent of the transformation.

Subdivisions claw their way up once cactus-studded ridgelines; gas stations, hotels, and restaurants crowd alongside what had been a dusty two-lane sweep of road, CA 62. RVs and pickups now rocket down the four-lane highway before pulling into ubiquitous trailer parks jammed with snowbirds and full-time residents; desert sprawls.

Even the shuttered automobile dealerships and half-empty strip-malls, ghostly remains of the 2007–2008 economic collapse, reinforced our unnerving realization of the thickening concrete imprint on this formerly clean, open, and sparse landscape.

How thick is reflected in the speed with which the desert—the Mojave and Sonoran (the latter is known locally as the Colorado Desert)—has urbanized. Cruise the I-10 corridor that splays along the southern border of

Joshua Tree National Park. Its growth rates are staggering. Palm Desert, inhabited by a mere 6,171 the last time we had been in the area, had jumped to 23,650 by 1990 and to nearly 50,000 in 2010. Indio blew up from 49,116 in 2000 to more than 76,000 ten years later; the 42,647 who called Cathedral City home in 2000 a decade later had swelled to more than 51,000. In the "City of Eternal Sunshine" (that would be Coachella), 40,000 have hunkered down, and Palm Springs now tops 44,000 people.

All these bodies, new and old, need shelter; they need water and energy; they require streets, stoplights, and schools, fire and police departments, hospitals. Work and shopping, entertainment and culture, no less than areas to recreate and play (golf, mostly): these make up but a partial list of the infrastructural requirements we demand of anyplace we inhabit.

The collective impact of these pressures can be intense for such an arid land. Trying to slake the unquenchable human thirst in a parched region is hard enough, for example, but it becomes a great deal more difficult when you mix in the conflicting ambitions of politicians and bureaucrats; developers, tribal leaders, and environmentalists; and ordinary residents.

Getting these interests, among many others, to agree on an equitable distribution of white gold, let alone to advance rigorous conservation measures that might sustain these still-booming communities well into the twenty-first century, will take time and patience.

But whether there is time enough is not clear. So I wondered while standing at the Oasis Visitor Center at the north entrance to J-Tree, listening to a canyon wren welcome the early morning light. One ornithologist likens the bird's seductive call to a "cascade of musical whistles," yet outside its lyrical song there wasn't a lot of water visible as I swung my binoculars to the west, focusing in on the San Bernardino Mountains; only the very highest peaks—notably, San Gorgonio—glistened.

Had this been a wet winter, there would have been a deeper snowpack and at much lower elevations; with the warm spring sun its melt already would have been tumbling down through the steep, sharp canyons cutting into the range's eastern slope, before spreading across the alluvial fans and then seeping underground to replenish the Mojave's sand aquifers (a slow transfer that the San Jacinto Mountains replicate for the Sonoran).

That process has been disrupted during the drought wracking the region since 2009. Since then, wintertime Pacific storms have shifted well to the north; should this drier pattern persist across the century, as most climate models predict, then local groundwater supplies will be in considerable jeopardy.

Add to this disquieting thought another: the American West in general has been experiencing mild winters; the Sierra and Wasatch have been reporting below-normal snowfall. Most worrisome for those who live in the Mojave are the Rockies, where the ski season has been abysmal.

However far away it may be, this range is more valuable to the metro desert than the nearby San Bernardinos and San Jacintos: its distant high-country snowfields are the source of the Colorado River, which since the 1930s has supplied the region with a steady flow through the California Aqueduct. The Metropolitan Water District, which operates the aqueduct's 242-mile-long network of dams, pumps, canals, tunnels, and pipes, provides the bulk of the water that residents of Palm Springs, Palm Desert, and Indio consume.

There is another warning sign, this too spotted at the Oasis Visitor Center. The site is so named because of the springs that once broke the surface here, a consequence of an impermeable barrier known as the Pinto Mountain fault: it blocks the underground flow of water coming off of the Queen Mountains, forcing it upwards to spill across the stony soil.

The native peoples who gathered around the springs—the Serrano, Chemehuevi, and Cahuilla—made good use of this critical resource to cultivate crops. This water also nourished California fan palms, whose wood fiber and fronds they wove into baskets and which sustained the animals they ate.

Understanding its value too were Anglo-American surveyors, explorers, and Forty-Niners who before the Civil War pushed across the desert. By the late nineteenth century, others began to set up camp in the area, hoping to exploit its mineral riches. Tapping the spring flow to wet their whistle, cool their animals, and fill their casks and canteens, or more industriously siphoning off its icy rush for mining operations, inevitably altered what the Serrano had called Mara, "a place of small springs and much grass." It became much less bountiful and bucolic.

To protect such stressed ecosystems, and the larger landscape of which they are a part, drove the tireless Minerva Hamilton Hoyt to advocate for a desert national park. Dubbed the Apostle of the Cacti, she earned this sobriquet for defending what most of her contemporaries dismissed as a wasteland, the disposable desert. Where some contemporaries saw only the sparkling riches that should be gouged out of its mountains, where others plucked its flowers and dug up Joshua Trees and other prickly mementos of their outback sojourn, Hoyt bore witness to a beauty integral to itself.

Preserving what she described as the Mojave's "silence and mystery" demanded a political solution. And shortly after the 1916 creation of the National Park system Hoyt started orchestrating a groundswell of support for congressional action to preserve her beloved terrain. Exhibits on desert flora and fauna; newspaper articles celebrating the stark beauty of this much-ignored environment; a letter-writing campaign to secure the requisite votes; coalition building: Hoyt's campaign was a classic example of how self-interest and public service can bring about social change, how a person of deep pockets and considerable skill can bend political power to her will.

Hoyt's chances of success, after more than a decade of activism, increased in February 1933, when during his final month in office President Herbert Hoover set a precedent for Joshua Tree with the creation of Death Valley National Monument. His successor, Franklin Roosevelt, a conservationist at heart, proved sympathetic and shrewd. He waited until August 1936, just days before the Labor Day start of his campaign for a second term, to invoke the powers given to him under the Antiquities Act, unilaterally establishing Joshua Tree National Monument. (The two national monuments became national parks in 1994, courtesy of the California Desert Protection Act.)

Alas, the newfound protections that park rangers brought to Joshua Tree's original 825,000 acres did little to save the Mara oasis. Instead, the creation of the national monument may have hastened its demise: the site drew even more visitors and residents to the desert, leading to accelerated pumping of local groundwater; by 1942 the spring had dried up. To recreate its life-giving flow, today the Park Service pipes water to the site, a trickle designed to feed a landscape that cannot function on its own.

The loss is not just ecological. It's also human. The original inhabitants of Joshua Tree, the agency concludes, had left the oasis by 1913. Their departure led a Smithsonian archaeologist to erase them from cultural memory, as if they had been swept away in a sandstorm: "Intrinsically, it is of little import who exercised sovereignty in this tract," he wrote in 1925; "to all purposes it was empty."

J. Smeaton Chase knew otherwise. In his 1919 *California Desert Trails*, a poetic meditation on his explorations of the deserts of Eastern California ("this bit of pure Arabia that has somehow fallen into our territory"), he offered up this sharp critique of the casual American displacement of the Other: "I do not know who owns the land, and, what is of more account, the water; but when I come upon these abandoned settlements of the Indians, at places where they would no doubt have wished to remain, I take them for links in an old but lengthening chain of wrong."

In the Mojave, some things never change.

Yosemite Constructed

Only a couple of thousand tourists trekked into Yosemite in 1871, yet they knew what they were coming to see; the sites they visited were predetermined, and their responses to them were prefelt. The magnificent valley may have been well off the beaten path, but its falls and domes and meadows were already "sites."

That's why these intrepid travelers had taken the trouble, and in the early 1870s it took some doing, to work their way up and over the rugged western slope of the Sierras and into what already had become a totemic terrain.

Alice Van Schaack was one of these pilgrims. When the twenty-seven-year-old New Yorker arrived late that July and caught her first glimpse of the valley below, she gave voice to a set of emotions that others before her (and many since) have expressed: drinking in the "wonderfully lovely scene," she later wrote her family, was a celestial experience. "Heaven itself could not have been much lovelier."

She had no reason to change her mind during her brief four-day stay. Hitting all the hot spots—Bridal Veil, "now a mere ribbon, while the Ribbon Fall itself is only observable by the dark outline its waters have left on the rock"; Yosemite Falls (which were dry); and Mirror Lake, "which we crossed in a leaky boat, and then waited patiently until its surface was undisturbed by a ripple, when we were rewarded by two perfect dissolving views of the North and South Domes."

About the slow-running falls, Nevada and Vernal, she wrote: although "we saw [them] at an unfavorable season, there was, however, a sufficient volume of water to give us pleasure, and I enjoyed watching the spray as it was blown down the stream. We then went on foot down a shorter trail . . . and had a fine view of the Vernal Fall from below. If you notice a lack of adjectives, please remember . . . I exhausted my stack in the valley."

As for the obligatory late-night observation of a moonrise, Alice waxed pious: "I shall never forget it, or indeed anything of interest connected with our trip; it was pure, unalloyed pleasure, such as we rarely taste in this life, but, I trust, may ever be ours in the world to come."

Her sentimental responses to her high-country adventure were heartfelt, if platitudinous. The religious origins of some of them are easy enough to discern, like Alice's sanctimonious remark after touring the Calaveras Grove (now Calaveras Big Trees State Park): "As I stood in [their] shadow . . . and thought of the many generations that had passed away during their existence, for a moment I felt insignificant in comparison, until I remembered that I am immortal, and they are not."

Less obvious is why she thought Yosemite would be a salve, why she wanted to travel so far to encounter its exotic beauties. Don't thank John Muir: he was in the valley when Alice was there, but they did not meet; his first published testimonial to Yosemite's grandeur would not appear until December 1871, five months after Van Schaack arrived.

Rather, Alice's guide was the intrepid James Mason Hutchings, who ran the hotel in which she and her party stayed (among its other guests were feminists Susan B. Anthony and Elizabeth Cady Stanton). Hutchings proved an amiable and attentive guide, leading his lodgers from one stellar location to another, educating them about their unique features, historic significance, and moral import (the latter of which, as you will have noticed, particularly attracted Alice).

She had met him in her family's parlor back in upstate New York, or at least she was introduced there to his literary persona: her family owned a copy of Hutchings's 1862 guidebook, *Scenes of Wonder and Curiosity in California*. She followed its recommendations for which routes to travel to the valley, a step-by-step choreography of the touristic experience there, to the letter.

Even Alice's post-Yosemite correspondence, which her brother would publish as *A Familiar Letter from a Daughter to Her Mother* (1871) and in which she recounted Hutchings's daily presence in the group's activities, contained references to the hotelier's writings so that her correspondents could follow her journey in their mind's eye: "As you will see by referring to the map, page 111, Hutchings's Yo-Semite Guide Book, we took the Coulterville trail, following the left bank of the crystal waters of the Merced. It is well named, for mercy is ever pure."

Thousands of other visitors, and the many more who only traveled to the Sierra in their imaginations, were as indebted to Hutchings's literal and figurative framing of this remarkable landscape. He made Yosemite *Yosemite*.

It is more precise to say he fabricated a certain version of Yosemite. Although much better known for his lengthy, and ultimately unsuccessful, court battle with the U.S. government to retain his claims to the land on which his hotel was constructed, it was Hutchings's construction of another sort that opened the way for the creation of the national park. For him "there was no contradiction in the idea that one could simultaneously feel a deep, spiritual connection to a place and seek to make a living in and from that place," making Hutchings one of the first to map out the intersection of conservationism and consumerism.

His career, Jen Huntley argues in *The Making of Yosemite* (2011), "illustrates the way that the Yosemite Grant [later park] and the environmental conservation movement it launched were integrally connected to and interdependent upon the consumer tourism that would be his bread and butter." Hutchings's actions on the ground and in print made it possible for such well-heeled visitors as Alice Van Schaack to revel in this remote playground.

The desire to see Yosemite, then, depended on and left behind a paper trail, archival litter that tells us a great deal about that era's cultural imagination, its reach and limitations, insight and blind spots. Yet for the park to become a tourist mecca (and later a national park) also required a tectonic shift in its demographics. The native peoples who lived and foraged along the valley, fished and hunted its creeks and rivers, meadows and woodlands, had to be expelled. This occurred in ways violent and exploitative, as the U.S. Army exerted its control over California after it became the thirty-first state in 1850. Their lives were crimped further as miners and speculators swarmed over the Sierra Mountains in search of gold, a rush that echoed across that century's middle decades and brought tens of thousands of migrants to California. Like locusts, they took over the land.

With them, too, came new technologies, among them the camera.

It is striking how quickly that once-cumbersome tool of representation and communication showed up in Yosemite. In June 1859, Charles Leander Weed snapped what is believed to be the area's first photograph, "The Yo-Semite Fall. 2500 feet high." What is even more noteworthy is that Weed's and the other early images became templates for all those that have been taken ever since.

Yosemite, after all, must be one of the most photographed places in North America. What the professional and amateur have captured on glass, film, or chip is predicated in good measure on the form, shape, and subject matter that Weed, Eadweard Muybridge, and Carleton Watkins, among others, focused their lenses on more than 150 years ago.

Because their photographs were widely disseminated, tourists who visited Yosemite in the mid-nineteenth century knew exactly what to look for. They were coming to experience up close what they had viewed from afar. Yet what these visitors and writers saw and felt, or more exactly what they were trained to visualize and project, is not all that was there.

A clue to what lies outside some of these texts' margins is embedded in Hutchings's 1886 *In the Heart of the Sierra*. Even as he inscribed Yosemite with much of its touristic significance, he also let slip some of its troubling backstory. As he led his readers step by step along what he dubbed the Mariposa Route, from San Francisco to Yosemite, Hutchings offers glimpses of the native peoples that the new economy displaced and of the immigrants—Chinese, Irish, and others—whose backbreaking labor eased the traveler's way.

The accompanying photographs offer another pattern. Only a few of them contain human beings, and those that do position them in such a way as to provide a sense of scale only. Big trees, steep cliffs, granite domes: the message is that this wilderness is empty, natural, profound. Devoid of the human stain, it is open to our projections—the most enduring and concerning of which is that wilderness is absent *of* us. In that negative is an admission of some of the enduring costs, human and environmental, associated with making this an exalted place.

So intense had this process become, so ingrained were its features, that when John Muir arrived in Yosemite for his first visit in 1868, he followed a well-beaten path. Consider the apocryphal story so beloved of his biographers about how this bearded, wide-eyed young man from Wisconsin learned of California's treasured landscape.

The narrative goes like this: after his arduous, life-changing thousand-mile tramp south to the Gulf of Mexico in 1867, during which he shook off the siren call of material wealth, Muir sailed to the Golden State. On the teeming streets of San Francisco, asked by an unknown passerby what he was looking for, Muir is said to have replied, "Anywhere wild."

That he was directed to Yosemite, by then well known to Americans east and west, urban and rural, suggests how tightly bound this wilderness was with the city he allegedly wished to escape. In time, Muir would forge these links ever more closely. What made him so palatable to the subsequent readers of his odes to Yosemite's wildness is how accessible he made its waterfalls and ragged cliffs, snowstorms, bright light, and crisp air. Thousands of "tired, nerve-shaken, over-civilized people are beginning to find out that going to the mountains is going home; that wildness is a necessity," he once asserted. It was an assertion that propelled ever more folks to travel to Yosemite, to consume its scenes and services.

Yes, he affected to disdain its hordes of visitors. "Only by going alone in silence, without baggage, can one truly get into the heart of the wilderness. All other travel is mere dust and hotels and baggage and chatter." Yet his inspiring words, like the early photographs, guidebooks, and lithographs, were directly responsible for these peoples' boisterous presence.

Their increasing numbers also helped elbow aside Yosemite's first peoples, the Miwok and Mono Indians; Muir announced they now were trespassing on what once had been their home ground. "Somehow they seemed to have no right place in the landscape," he wrote after one encounter with a group of Mono in high country, "and I was glad to see them fading out of sight down the pass."

Fade out: this photographic metaphor codifies what "John of the Mountains" and his contemporaries believed was the necessary, because inevitable, transition from barbarism to civilization. They institutionalized this expulsion as they fought successfully to turn Yosemite into a national park, a battle in which John Muir played a formative role.

That said, this effort to exclude some and include others—to make Yosemite white—had been initiated long before Muir joined the fray. It was a consequence of the mid-nineteenth-century push to survey Yosemite's geological past, map its topography, and through the printed word and illustrative image lay claim to its snow-kissed mountains, thunderous cataracts, and wildflower-waving leas. As critic W. J. T. Mitchell has asserted, landscape photography "is a particular historical formation associated with European imperialism."

That is not how Muir would have understood what he and his friends who were artists and photographers were doing when they set out to capture Yosemite's beguiling beauty. For Muir, who trafficked in the language of the ecstatic, it was in nature alone that Americans (and a lot of others) would be reborn.

Their spiritual renewal would come through direct contact with the glacier-carved Range of Light, a divine sanctuary Muir believed only could be appreciated through individual tests of will. His "wilderness was a much more immersive experience for those who would adopt it," Jen Huntley notes, "replacing the act of viewing and 'reading' landscape scenery for its 'intrinsic' messages with the act of toiling in high mountain places to cultivate a relationship with the sacred."

Seeking higher ground was also a way to shed the grinding materialism of industrial society. "Muir taught generations of readers to seek solitude in Nature," Huntley affirms, and "to understand wilderness not only as separate from but morally . . . superior to 'base' human activity." There's nothing so modern as Muir's antimodernism.

Nothing may be more damaging, too. Huntley, for instance, makes a strong case for critiquing Muir's articulation of a binary world in which the human is inimical to the natural—and employs Hutchings as her foil. To do so, she makes extensive use of historian William B. Cronon's insights, laid out in his now-iconic essay "The Trouble with Wilderness": Muir's call of the wild offers a "flight from history, in its siren song of escape, in its reproduction of the dangerous dualism that sets human beings outside of nature." As such, Cronon concludes, "wilderness poses a serious threat to responsible environmentalism."

By contrast, Hutchings may offer an antidote for what ails us (and the planet). While he "lived and worked in Yosemite," Huntley writes, he "strove to weave together his sense of Yosemite's sacred value with a daily life built on local resources." In seeking to educate his readers about nature's sublime values and make a decent living at the same time, Hutchings adopted a small-is-beautiful approach that speaks volumes to this climate-changed era. "If we are to imagine our own sustainable future," Huntley writes, the critical first step will be to find "a way to marry our aesthetic and spiritual appreciation for the value of nature with our need to flourish."

Achieving that difficult balance requires a searching, inward look, not unlike that moment when Alice Van Schaack gazed upon Mirror Lake—"the most exquisite sight, I think, we saw in our wanderings." As its waters stilled, and the trees above, which formed "a fringe of living green," swam into view, she recalled "the Claude Lorraine glass, Mr. [George W.] King, the artist," had shown her the day before. Peering into its solid dark convex form, adjusting to the diminished scale it produced, Alice glimpsed her proper place in the landscape.

"Between Dark Wall and Wild Throng"

Yosemite gave me nightmares. Each night, for four nights, I woke up startled and disoriented. What had jolted me awake was the howling of coyotes, a pack whose raucous voices sounded like a group of tipsy teenagers screeching in a darkened tunnel. But the real haunting, the panic I escaped from by way of the coyotes' hair-raising calls, was human.

My dreams were filled with people dying, in ways terrifying and terrible. Real people. Like Kent Butler, who in mid-May 2011, after climbing up Mist Trail to Vernal Falls, had slipped close to the bottom and skidded down a rock and into the raging, frigid Merced River. On July 19, after clambering over a guardrail at the edge of Vernal Falls where it plunges 317 feet into the granite boulders that had claimed Butler's life two months earlier, Hormiz David, Ramina Badal, and Ninos Yacoub were swept away. Twelve days later, and hours before my wife and I arrived in the national park, Haley LaFlamme lost her footing while descending the vertiginous, rain-slick steps chipped into Half Dome, plunging six hundred feet to her death. On our last afternoon, as one search-and-rescue team recovered

Hormiz David's body from the still-swollen Merced, we watched another transfer an unconscious Kao Kue, badly injured on Mist Trail, to a yellow medevac helicopter that had landed on the Ahwahnee meadow; the teenager was ferried to a distant hospital (where he later died).

These horrific stories were shared at breakfast, bandied across picnic tables, overheard during candlelit dinners; they hung in the air like the pall of smoke swirling up from the Avalanche Fire, stinging and acrid. Little wonder that I transmuted these lost souls' final screams into the coyotes' shocking wail.

That is not how John Muir would have us think of death. Not in his beloved Yosemite. Close study of nature's ways there led him to conclude on an upbeat note: "No particle of her material is wasted or worn-out. It is eternally flowing from use to use, beauty to yet higher beauty; and we soon cease to lament waste and death, and rather rejoice and exult in the imperishable unspendable wealth of the universe."

Resurrection was the primary principle in Muir's cosmology, an impulse that my eldest sister, an Episcopal minister, likens to her flock's eagerness to skip Good Friday so as to get to the good news of Easter.

But then Muir was reborn in Yosemite, and ever after proclaimed its holiness. His words about the jagged landscape's divinity, its eternal peace, became scripture—part Bible, part Baedeker. And they energized the movement to preserve Yosemite as a national park. Now the

National Park Service makes devoted use of his journal jottings, philosophical musings, and giddy affirmations about its manifold blessings to affirm and shape its many visitors' experiences.

The agency especially likes this aphorism I spotted while browsing in the Yosemite Valley Visitor Center: "Thousands of tired, nerve-shaken, over-civilized people are beginning to find out that going to the mountains is going home; that wildness is a necessity." Other such homilies hang on banners tacked to the rough walls of the Tuolumne Meadows Visitor Center. There, too, you'll find a reverential wooden plaque that reads: "In 1868, a young naturalist named John Muir came to Yosemite in search of a 'wild place.' After ten years of wandering and studying he left to become the most influential conservationist of his time. And although the Sierra was no longer his home, this range always remained his place of spiritual renewal. What drew Muir to these mountains and what legacy has he left us?"

The marker, with its sermonic tone and didactic close, answers its own question and underscores it with the accompanying carved image of the weary-eyed prophet, complete with streaming hair and long beard. Muir's our Moses, leading us to the Promised Land.

So when he tells us that death is natural, beautiful, I get it; or at least I get why he thought so. Walk along the handily named John Muir Trail as it parallels and then crosses the upper reaches of the Tuolumne, and even the dust you kick up seems purified in the subalpine air. Stick your feet into the river's chilled rush; lift your face to the brilliant warm-blue sky; breathe in the needle-sharp scent of mountain hemlock and lodgepole pine. Everything is clean. Elemental.

It is that essential clarity that Muir sought in the Sierra, the Range of Light. It is also why he became fixated on "dazzling bright" glaciers, why in their study this self-styled "moral wanderer" anticipated getting as "near to the heart of the world as I could." His journeys would be filled with peril. But Muir found compensation in mortal danger: "I have often felt that to meets one's fate in the heart of a glacier," he wrote in *The Stickeen* (1909), a tale about his adventures in Alaska, "would be blessed compared with death . . . from a shabby lowland accident."

He had a chance to test that sentiment in October 1872, during a rigorous ascent of icy Mount Ritter, "king of the mountains of the middle portion of the High Sierra, as Shasta of the north and Whitney of the south." On his approach, he was confronted with "a glacier swooping down" the mountain's face nearly to his feet, "then curving westward and pouring its frozen flood into a dark blue lake, whose shores were bound with precipices of crystalline snow." Crossing it was the first of his worries: "The entire front above the glacier appeared as one tremendous precipice, slightly receding at the top, and bristling with spires and pinnacles set above one another in formidable array. Massive lichen-stained battlements stood forward here and there, hacked at the top with angular notches, and separated by frosty gullies and recesses that have been veiled in shadow ever since their creation; while to right and left, as far as I could see, were huge, crumbling buttresses, offering no hope to the climber."

He pushed on, only to discover that the mountain itself was "a wilderness of crumbling spires and battlements, built together in bewildering combinations, and glazed in many places with a thin coating of ice, which I had to hammer off with stones."

Muir knew he could not descend—"for, so steep was the entire ascent, one would inevitably fall to the glacier in case a single misstep were made"; his way forward was just as treacherous. As he picked his way up an avalanche channel, suddenly he was "brought to a dead stop, with arms outspread, clinging close to the face of the rock, unable to move hand or foot either up or down. My doom appeared fixed. I must fall. There would be a moment of bewilderment, and then a lifeless rumble down the one general precipice to the glacier below."

Although he was "nerve-shaken for the first time since setting foot on the mountains," this "terrible eclipse" suddenly, miraculously abated: "Life blazed forth again with preternatural clearness. I seemed suddenly to become possessed of a new sense." Muir's "trembling muscles became firm again, every rift and flaw in the rock was seen as through a microscope, and my limbs moved with a . . . precision with which I seemed to have nothing at all to do. Had I been borne aloft upon wings, my deliverance could not have been more complete."

If only those who fell to their deaths in Yosemite in summer 2011 had been as fortunate.

Gila Wild

The most famous wolf to trot through the pages of American nature writing died at the hands of Aldo Leopold. Years later, in *A Sand County Almanac* (1949), one of the sacred texts of the modern environmental movement, Leopold revived the mother wolf and her cubs and relived the moment when, "full of trigger-itch," he and his comrades pumped round after round into the "melee of wagging tails and playful maulings." His then-youthful rationale—"In those days we had never heard of passing up a chance to kill a wolf"—no longer convinced him. Leopold would recall climbing down the steep rimrock to where the mortally wounded wolf lay, just "in time to watch a fierce green fire dying in her eyes," a haunting vision. Maybe Henry David Thoreau was right, he mused; instead of extirpating the untamed, we should recognize that in "wildness is the salvation of the world."

This catalytic incident is thought to have occurred on the Apache National Forest in north-central Arizona. However, it was in southwestern New Mexico, on the Gila National Forest, that the famed conservationist would act on his emerging understanding of the value of wilderness preservation. Before doing so, Leopold conferred with Arthur Carhart, the Forest Service's first landscape architect, about Carhart's plan to preserve the unspoiled nature of Trapper's Lake on the White River National Forest. Drawing on Carhart's ideas for inspiration, in 1921 Leopold published what amounted to a declaration of first principles. "By 'wilderness,' I mean a continuous stretch of country preserved in its natural state, open to lawful hunting and fishing, big enough to absorb a two weeks' pack trip, and kept devoid of roads, artificial trails, cottages, or other works of man."

Even in the 1920s, not many places would meet all these qualifications, but the upper watershed of the Gila River did. Its typography—"mountain ranges and box canyons"—had isolated it from development, Leopold affirmed, leaving it in a "semi-virgin state." Its relatively pristine character made it perfect for his purposes: The Gila was the "last typical wilderness in the southwestern mountains. Highest use demands its preservation." With the support of Forest Service chief William B. Greeley and regional forester Frank Pooler, he submitted a proposal to designate the vast region a wilderness. To that end, on June 3, 1924, the Forest Service set aside 755,000 acres, the world's first such designation; appropriately, a portion of it today bears Leopold's name.

Embedded in Leopold's remarkable legacy is a core assumption: that wilderness is absent of, and an antidote to, civilization, a place separate and apart from human impress. This idea emerged in the late nineteenth century in response to the industrial revolution and rapid urbanization. Writers such as John Muir asserted that the call of the wild, of open space, would be a tonic for those living in cramped, dense cities. This notion only makes sense, however, in the context of other historic forces that had emptied these lands of the people who once lived within them.

The Gila wildlands, which Leopold encountered in the early 1920s and which today draw thousands of hikers every year to test themselves against the site's sheer cliffs, towering mesas, and frigid waters, is devoid of people as a direct result of the Mexican-American War and the Gadsden Purchase of 1853. To manifest its control over the region, the U.S. Army ultimately defeated the Apache and relocated them to reservations. Even with their forced removal, evidence remained that what would become a wilderness had supported a series of complex societies dating back to the Paleo-Indian peoples who occupied the Gila highlands roughly 11,000 years ago. When the subsequent Cochise and Mogollon cultures disappeared sometime in the thirteenth century, they too left behind a built environment that included cliff dwellings and pueblos, and a material culture rich in pottery (remnants of which have been preserved in Gila Cliff Dwellings National Monument, located within the national forest). The Apaches, who arrived three hundred years later, held this ground for several centuries. To declare this land wild, then, has been to erase these people and their past, an erasure that the Gila designation set in motion in 1924 and has been replicated wherever wilderness has been proclaimed.

Excluding fire from the Gila has been a more difficult proposition than ignoring its human history. In response to the 1910 Big Burn, which consumed millions of acres in Washington, Idaho, and Montana, the Forest Service committed itself to suppressing blazes wherever possible. Even though by midcentury foresters in the South would challenge this orthodoxy after learning that longleaf pine was fire-dependent, meaning flames are essential to creating the conditions for its regeneration, their Western counterparts did not accept this new concept for several decades. Intriguingly, it was on the Gila Wilderness in 1975 that the agency first reintroduced fire. After research revealed that old-growth ponderosa pine, a dominant species in the forest, "germinated, established, and lived most of their lives under the effects of repeated fire," the Forest Service experimented with allowing lightning-ignited fires to burn or setting prescribed fires to replicate historic fire regimes on the forest. This pathbreaking decision led to a new emphasis on ecological restoration—on managing *with* fire, not against it, a policy that received its most significant test with the 2012 Whitewater-Baldy conflagration.

That fire—one journalist called it a "flaming tornado"—torched 297,845 acres, mostly in the wilderness area, the single largest in New Mexico history. But the vast size of the blaze is less important than the severity of the burn, and because of forty years of deliberate fire management within the Gila, the Whitewater-Baldy was considerably less intense than it might have been, a mark of a healthy ecosystem.

Accepting that fire is not the enemy of but a tool necessary for good forestry is a reflection of an attitude Leopold had urged Americans to adopt, "an intelligent humility toward man's place in nature." Accepting a less elevated status comes with the recognition that while we "live in a world of wounds," many of which are self-inflicted, our task is to bind them up—as Leopold modeled when he successfully pushed for the creation of the Gila Wilderness Area.

Is Nothing Sacred?

The falcon flew low and fast over Strawberry Rock, an outcropping high above the Rio Brazos Valley, just east of Chama, New Mexico.

We were sharing a picnic with good friends in a pine copse rooted in rough sandstone and marveling over the clear blue horizon, when the small raptor shot past; its backswept wings and breakneck speed were its only identifiable features.

As it stretched out and banked west, the falcon's swift form was highlighted against the quartzite face of Brazos Cliff, glowing in the midday sun; it then hurtled down the dark green valley, following the silvery flow west toward the Rio Chama.

That shutter-click of a moment seemed suspended in time. Like our vacation, a lifting up and out, a release.

Yet at some point the falcon had to wing home, and so did we, though our pace was a bit more sedate. A day later we were rolling along U.S. 64 across northwestern New Mexico, straight through the state's oil-and-gas patch in the San Juan River watershed.

The region contains the nation's second largest gas reserves, a play that has gone through a series of booms and busts since the 1920s, but it has been experiencing a decline of late. The small towns along our route bear the marks of this economic withering—idled rigs, banged-up pickups, pitted roadbeds, and dusty stores with little on the shelves. Even the relatively bustling Farmington, which received a substantial infusion of American Reinvestment and Recovery Act dollars to repave an extensive portion of U.S. 64, has not been able to generate enough new work to break out of its doldrums.

That's why so many are looking for salvation in two words: Mancos Shale. The formation, which extends from New Mexico into portions of Colorado, Utah, and Wyoming, is buried about a mile beneath the surface. Estimated to contain upwards of 6 billion barrels of oil, approximately one-third of which lies within New Mexico, the untapped resource is being touted as a godsend for the recession-hit area.

At a March 2013 conference on this deposit's tantalizing possibilities, T. Greg Merrion, president of Merrion Oil and Gas, exulted: "I'm bullish on the Mancos. We've already seen a number of wells drilled that are economic. I'm looking forward to this next boom." Former U.S. senator Pete Domenici was just as giddy: "These are happy times again."

Don't break out the bunting quite so quickly. It might be years before energy companies are convinced that they can profitably extract oil and gas through the horizontal drilling and hydraulic fracturing techniques that have been responsible for the explosive productivity in the Eagle Ford play in south Texas, the Baaken in South Dakota, and the Marcellus in Pennsylvania and West Virginia. It will take time, too, for the Bureau of Land Management to develop the requisite environmental impact assessments for air and water quality. And should the run begin, its proponents will have to contend with an energized and skeptical citizenry unconvinced that the boom's economic benefits will outweigh its social costs and environmental deficits.

One of the flashpoints already has been identified— Chaco Culture National Historic Park. Although a number of other parks are under threat, including the Delaware Water Gap, as well as Theodore Roosevelt, Yellowstone, and Glacier National Parks, Chaco Culture is particularly vulnerable. The 34,000-acre site encompasses the largest set of extant Chacoan ruins, which date back at least a millennium and contain a remarkable set of masonry structures that served its inhabitants as a ritual, ceremonial, and communal center for three hundred years or so. Pueblo Bonito, for instance, is thought to have been the world's largest apartment building, housing upwards of thirteen hundred people, a size not eclipsed until the late 1880s.

The first step in conserving these edifices occurred in March 1907: President Theodore Roosevelt used his authority under the Antiquities Act, adopted the year before, to throw the mantel of federal protection over the archaeological marvels. They are "of extraordinary interest because of their number and their great size," the official proclamation reads, "and because of the innumerable and valuable relics of a prehistoric people which they contain, and it appears that the public good would be promoted by preserving these prehistoric remains as a National Monument."

Like many of the other sites of American antiquity that Roosevelt and his immediate successors denoted as national monuments, Chaco Culture had been looted and vandalized. The depredations there and elsewhere were so egregious that they led archaeologists, anthropologists, and concerned citizens to pressure Congress to pass what became the Antiquities Act.

Unfortunately, the new law did not stop the pilfering of these prehistoric gems, as there was no consistent management and policing of the area until the National Park Service, which was not founded until 1916, took over responsibility for Chaco Culture and its peer parks. Even then, a lax form of what historian Hal K. Rothman called "Warning Sign" preservationism prevailed until the 1930s, when the southwestern national monuments experienced more sustained oversight.

Chaco Culture received increased renown in 1987 after UNESCO tapped it as a World Heritage Site, praising its builders' achievements: "The Chaco people combined

preplanned architectural designs, astronomical align-
ments, geometry, landscaping and engineering to create
an ancient urban center of spectacular public architecture."

Sensitive preservation of the surviving portions of
this sprawling complex is a real challenge under ordinary
circumstances—the footprints of even the most respectful
visitors can compromise the site's archaeological integrity.
Now the earthen remnants of this ancient civilization face
a much greater threat due to the unsettling reality that
they overlie the Mancos Shale formation.

Since the turn of this century, the BLM has been
actively engaged with energy companies scouring the
San Juan basin for untapped reservoirs of oil and gas. In
2008–2009—and not for the first time—it offered leases
on eight parcels totaling 10,000 acres near Chaco Culture,
only to pull them off the table when the Hopi challenged
the offering. In 2013 the BLM revived the stalled project,
an announcement that raised another hue and cry. Tribal
authorities, local environmental groups such as the Chaco
Alliance, and the National Parks Conservation Association weighed in. In the face of this concerted opposition,
the agency once more withdrew the leases from auction.

No one expects that this will be the final clash over
the energy locked deep beneath Chaco Culture; it has a
competing value that will lead to future wrangles, though
opponents gained some time during winter 2015 as the
cost of energy plummeted and oil fields everywhere shut
down wells and thousands of workers lost their jobs.

Yet when the issue is revived—and it will be in New Mexico as elsewhere—the political context in which these future debates over Chaco Canyon's fate will occur has shifted, and dramatically so. Across the state, more communities and counties are responding to deep-seated worries about the inimical impact of fracking on public health and on the sacred lands and cultural resources that define this Land of Enchantment.

A newspaper box offered my first clue to the extent of the opposition. Stopping in Bloomfield to stretch our legs and gas up—yes, the irony is inescapable—I peered through the scratched Plexiglas to read the front page of the *Farmington Daily Times*. It contained a major story about the ongoing controversy surrounding Chaco Culture, and a quick search online brought up similar stories from other New Mexico towns such as Las Vegas; since 2012, it too has been battling over the legality of prohibiting fracking within the city's limits.

County commissioners have been busy as well. Worried about the damage that hydraulic fracturing will do to local groundwater in this arid land, and responding to the mounting evidence that this explosive technique has been responsible for the sharp uptick in earthquakes in the region, Mora County instituted an outright ban against fracking in May 2012, becoming the first county in the nation to institute a permanent injunction. Citizens and politicians in Colfax and Santa Fe Counties were also contemplating what actions they might take, and San Miguel

County has had a moratorium on fracking for several years.

Grassroots organizing and community ordinances aimed at stymieing the power of megacorporations and their political minions are inevitably tough battles. The difficulties will only intensify should the Mancos Shale formation come under rapid exploitation.

But I also wouldn't bet against those defending one of the spiritual epicenters of the southwestern ancient life and fighting to protect their right, and that of succeeding generations, to drink pure water and breathe clean air.

Galvanic and proactive, these activists' declaration of an alternative vision of homeland security is also a daring act of imagination—every bit as riveting as a fleet falcon in flight.

Still Grand

The Grand Canyon has the unnerving capacity to shut us up.

Native peoples have lived in and around it for millennia, with varying degrees of intimacy. For many of them it has served as sacred ground from whence life began; approachable on pilgrimage, held at a distance. Others, such as the Havasupai and Hualapai, have lived comfortably within its contours for centuries.

Not so the Spanish: when its explorers arrived in 1540, they took one look around and skedaddled—and no European came back for another two hundred years or so.

One of those who explored this riparian labyrinth was John Wesley Powell. In 1869, with a small crew, he led an expedition down the Colorado River, the erosive power of which had been cutting through layers of sediment for millions of years. As he ran its rapids, mapped its breadth, volume, and length, and ogled its staggering geological record encompassing 2 billion years, his scientific lexicon failed him. Only a biblical metaphor would do: the Grand Canyon was earth's Book of Revelation.

Forester Gifford Pinchot had a similar response. In 1891, he walked up to the canyon's south rim, and, lo and behold, the usually gregarious young man could not speak. "Awe-struck and silent, I strove to grasp the vastness and beauty of the greatest sight this world has to offer." On impulse, he began to sing the Doxology—"Praise God, from whom all blessings flow"—a spiritual spell that his guide, a fellow by the name of Doran, broke with his repeated mantra: "My, ain't it pretty." At that instant, Pinchot laughed later, "I wanted to throw him in."

How are we to comprehend this spellbinding chasm that puts us at such a loss for words? Since the late nineteenth century, one tool artists have adopted in an attempt to bridge this gap between the emotional and verbal, and to communicate the canyon's mystery and meaning, has been the camera. Their adoption of this technology of representation, historian Finis Dunaway argues in *Natural Visions*, a superb look at environmental image-making, was not (and is not) solely aesthetic.

In their steady hands, figures such as Ansel Adams and Eliot Porter sought to shape the American imagination, sculpting our responses to and need for the wild. Working from within this artistic tradition is a new generation of photographers, a sampling of whose work makes up the core of the Smithsonian Institution's traveling exhibition *Lasting Light: 125 Years of Grand Canyon Photography*.

In collaboration with the Grand Canyon Association, and curated by the photographic staff at Eastman

Kodak and National Geographic, the show contains sixty stunning photographs, beautifully reproduced, well displayed, and nicely contextualized. As a bonus, many of the images are accompanied by their creators' oft-stammered explanations for their decision to turn their gaze on the indescribable.

Like the canyon, the exhibit is crowded with surprises. Begin with its title panel, whose backdrop is Robert McDonald's striking photograph *Ships Sailing in Fog*. The production of that singular photograph is as remarkable as the image itself.

The day in question was hardly optimal: gale-force winds howled across the southern rim; buffeted, McDonald held his ground, waiting for the perfect light, for shade, hue, and image to line up just right, as if in a crosshair. When it happened, his 4-by-5 camera caught a late afternoon glimpse of the canyon's iconic landmarks—Solomon Temple, Angel's Gate, Zoroaster Temple, Shiva Temple.

In a sense, his photograph is a trope, an expected visual of the stacked layering of canyon walls and exposed outcroppings that recede into the background. A nice added touch is the mist that swirls around these hard-rock facades, softening them with what seems to be a translucent film, a scrim.

What seems an ethereal fog was in fact smog. The particulate matter came from as far away as Los Angeles and as close as the towering stacks rising above the power plants in Arizona's Four Corners (which produce some of the City of Angels' energy). Their combined soot befouled the viewshed of an inspiring landscape whose virtues President Theodore Roosevelt challenged his generation to defend: "In the Grand Canyon, Arizona has a natural wonder which, so far as I know, is in kind absolutely unparalleled throughout the rest of the world," he declared in May 1903. "I want to ask you to do one thing in connection with it in your own interest and in the interest of the country—to keep this great wonder of nature as it now is."

And also to pay it forward, he urged, after signing legislation establishing the canyon as an inviolable national monument, "so that your children's children will get the benefit of it." The whirl of particulate matter in McDonald's photo confirms we have mishandled this intergenerational responsibility.

Yet the source of pollution, curiously enough, offers Southern Californians the chance for reparation. As the car drives, Grand Canyon National Park is roughly five hundred miles from the Los Angeles Basin, but despite that distance the prevailing breezes intimately bind us to the cavernous site. McDonald's image becomes a mirror in which we can see the deleterious consequences of our auto-fixed culture, an insight that might help us turn the corner, becoming better stewards of the air and land, here and there.

Adding to that reflective prospect is the seductive capacity of the photographic lens to open our eyes to the canyon's flood of light, an illuminating power to wow.

That was an inescapable conclusion I reached several years ago after my wife and I slowly explored the jammed-packed exhibition and its display of the work of twenty-six contemporary photographers. The collection rocked our senses.

Colors: turquoise and tangerine, sandstone, blood-orange red, blinding white, ochre and lavender, washed limestone, and needle green; crystalline blue, liquid amber.

Smells: which you cannot inhale but somehow waft off the prints—rain on sunbaked stone; sticky pine resin; snow on chilled cone.

Movement: river rush, dust whorls, eddied backwater, fading contrails.

Feel: pitch-dark silence, slivered moon; a bighorn in silhouette.

"Mood is what elicits impact and emotion," observes Jack Dykinga, many of whose photographs graced the show. Creating that deeper, affective response is what he and his peers shoot for: "Ansel Adams said that when you can not only show someone a place, but let them feel what you felt that's the highest mark of success."

They do so not with a panoramic sweep so beloved of their nineteenth-century predecessors, whose wide-angled effort to encompass all ended up shrinking their massive subject. Instead, the modern photographers tend to frame their field of vision more tightly, making the small seem voluminous.

At this, Gary Ladd is particularly effective. *Reflection, Mouth of Cathedral Wash* is a beguiling abstract of gravel, rock, and water. A snapshot in miniature of the elemental forces that over eons have made the canyon grand; a delicate composition of geologic energy unleashed. But peering closely at a pool of water reveals in its flat surface a solar-lit reflection of the jagged walls above, a scale set in earthen time.

Then there is Dugald Bremner's *Boats on the Water, Marble Canyon*: an eerie scene in which the dory in question, its oars and huddled passengers illuminated with light emanating from stage left, appears to be floating on air, a trompe l'oeil effect courtesy of the thick craggy shadow cast up on the facing canyon wall. A moment of little moment, perhaps, except that Bremner has given it an intensely meditative feel.

So too for some of Liz Hymans's diminutive images—*Sculptured Schist*, in which metamorphic rock that the sediment-rich river has worn down and grooved is caught so that it looks like a Henry Moore abstraction; *Sacred Dátura*, a close-up of its pinwheeled flower, reminds immediately of Georgia O'Keeffe.

It also contains an echo of Aldo Leopold. In *A Sand County Almanac*, he writes a prayerful ode to *Draba*, a tiny flower with a short life cycle. "He who hopes for spring with upturned eyes never sees so small a thing as *Draba*. He who despairs of spring with downcast eye steps on it, unknowing.

He who searches for spring with his knees in the mud finds it, in abundance." For Leopold and Hymans, the singular contains the multitude; the petite evokes the whole.

In this declaration of nature's universality, this faith that everything is connected (thanks, Emerson), in the presumption that all we need to do is to look carefully to identify the tissue of associations, lay the exhibit's most poignant claim; this exhibition is not entitled *Lasting Light* for nothing.

Even the deft framing of the individual photographs—borders that contain and restrain—contributes to the feeling we can know what we see, even of a place as inexpressibly immense as the Grand Canyon. We can transcend this place.

Eliot Porter did not share such confidence. No photographer did more to express his adoration of nature's wildness to a midcentury audience hungry for such evocations. Yet in 1960 when he rafted down the Colorado à la John Wesley Powell, he was "overwhelmed by the scenery—both in prospect and in description grossly underrated."

Nothing he had read or seen prepared him for what he encountered as he floated along the river's rush. "The monumental structure of the towering walls," he wrote, "defied comprehension. I didn't know where to look, what to focus on, and in my confusion, photographic opportunities slipped by." His admission of failure is comforting. Surely it is a good thing that some experiences resist our studied effort to comprehend them, that some scenes leave us speechless.

Rocky Mountain High

Fern Lake. The very name beguiles, with its promise of soft green and cold blue, an alpine tableau high up in Rocky Mountain National Park.

A pacific landscape, one might think, and according to Enos Mills, the park's creative genius, that is how we are supposed to respond to it. After all, establishing such a sanctuary was the central reason he and others fought for the park's preservation.

"A National Park is an island of safety in this riotous world," he averred in *Your National Parks*, published two years after President Woodrow Wilson signed the park into law in 1915. "Splendid forests, the waterfalls that leap in glory, the wild flowers that charm and illuminate the earth, the wild sheep of the sky-line crags, and the beauty of the birds, all have places of refuge which parks provide."

Those humans in greatest need of this respite, Mills declared, were the swelling number of people crowding into early twentieth-century cities, a sickly lot who would be invigorated by close contact with nature's salubrious scenery. "Blue Monday did not originate outdoors."

Maybe his claim for the virtues of high-country serenity was what led a gaggle of us to gather in the park for a long-overdue reunion. Perhaps that is why we fixed on a trail called Fern Lake. It seemed to offer peace and quiet.

Peaceful, it was. Quiet, not so much—this is a voluble crew. Still, we fell silent at the trailhead while reading a notice suggesting that whatever else we might see on the sun-drenched, pine-scented hike, we'd need to adjust our chromatic scale, factoring in more browns, blacks, and grays.

WARNING: A wildfire burned through this area
Be alert for the following potential hazards

- Falling trees and limbs
- Unstable slopes and rolling material
- Burned out stump holes
- Areas that still may be smoldering
- Bridges and other trail structures that may be damaged
- Off-trail travel is not recommended in burned areas

The sign did not lie. Even as we climbed up the rutted trail through stands of mature ponderosa pine, picked our way over lichen-stained boulders, and spotted a mountain bluebird darting into a spray of long, thin needles, even while resting by a thunderous white-rushed cataract, the markers of fire were inescapable.

Across the valley to our south we glimpsed intensely burned acres whose wind-blown brands had sailed across the lake below to land in the high ground we were moving through. The damage here was patchy. Like sentinels, individual trees—some crisp black, others singed so badly that their needles had turned a bright orange—stood out in stark relief among those that had escaped the blasting heat; others lay crown down on the rocky slope, like tumbled tombstones.

A pungent aroma, a mere hint at first, strengthened as later we swung down Cub Lake trail; you could almost taste the smoke. The pathway scrambles just below a ridgeline and within minutes we found ourselves in a moonscape of carbonized trees—canted, twisted, and toppled. All that remained of the small bridge spanning Wuh Creek, gushing that day with snowmelt, was an unsteady metal frame. Everywhere, the soil appeared to have been vaporized, the humus and the microbes it sustained incinerated.

Even so, along the creek's banks new growth was pushing up, fresh foliage capturing the sun's energy to fuel the growth of its roots that would help it anchor itself more firmly in the stony ground. Bit by bit, this complex process of photosynthesis is allowing the forest to recover, from understory to canopy.

Fire's regenerative agency was not uppermost on the minds of firefighters in late November when the Fern Lake fire of 2012 tore through the Cub Lake district.

Seven weeks earlier, the blaze had begun in Forest Canyon through which the Big Thompson River cuts. Seen from above, a vantage point we would gain the next day from a scenic pullout along Trail Ridge Road, the canyon is a sweep of orange, green, and red. Two reciprocal forces have been reshaping the forest that stretched beneath our feet. The bark beetle infestation has devastated the drainage, as it has across the state; and the Rockies, like the rest of the West, has been reeling from years of drought.

Into this tinder-dry situation walked a camper. The National Park Service suspected that this individual lit an illegal fire whose flames were not doused well enough or which escaped. In any event, on October 9 smoke was spotted, downwind campgrounds and trails were evacuated, and the agency and its firefighting partners began to map out the best way to manage the burn.

Management was complicated by the severe conditions on the ground. This particular canyon had not burned in over eight hundred years (a not unusual condition for high-elevation woodlands). The absence of fire had made the canyon floor quite impenetrable, too.

Estimating that the pine beetles had killed more than half the standing trees, the Park Service also worried about the hazards firefighters would face if they were airlifted into the area where the "dead and down fuel layer . . . exceeds twenty feet deep." Gaining a foothold in this treacherous terrain would be impossible, and would be made all the more unstable given the powerful winds that regularly buffet the steep-walled valley. Forest Canyon was a firetrap.

For the next month and a half, firefighters did what they could, fighting along the periphery of what was a relatively small fire of fifteen hundred acres or so, using ridges to anchor their firebreaks, and where possible making use of water-dropping planes and helicopters, although air turbulence and the tight canyon limited their utility.

This safety-first strategy was sorely tested during the evening of November 30 as strong winds careened down Forest Canyon, reenergizing the fire. Within thirty-five minutes, its flames raced out three miles, more than doubling the acreage consumed. Its advance into low-lying Bear Lake and Moraine Park was only slowed after firefighters sparked backfires. The flames were smothered several days later by a snowstorm, but not before they had torched the Cub Lake watershed, making skeletal what was once arboreal beauty.

So unusual was this conflagration that at first blush it does not seem relevant to other settings. After all, this blaze erupted outside what is considered the Rockies' fairly short fire season and thereby offered a serious challenge to its successful suppression.

Each September, according to Park Service reports, "the fire community enters into its 'shoulder season.' During this time, as with many seasonal occupations, staffing begins to reduce dramatically, leaving relatively few resources available by October. Additionally, equipment such as helicopters and planes are less available as they are being serviced and maintained for the next year's season." Consequently, the agency had to get creative about securing a funding stream and establishing new interagency partnerships to cobble together air support, a process that "took much longer than usual."

Yet this worst-case scenario might be the new normal.

If so, we might also be forced to give up the idea that there is an off-season for fire. Across the West, regardless of elevation, fires are erupting earlier, running longer, and intensifying in force. Consider the explosive firestorms that ripped through Ventura County's coastal range in April and May 2013 and acted like October infernos, consuming bone-dry vegetation; CalFire reported that the Golden State was on a record pace for the number of wildfires, and the summer had only just started.

Colorado was also under siege. The ferocity of the Black Forest Fire and West Fork blaze in the Centennial State's southern mountains, like the devastatingly fatal Yarnell Hill fire in Arizona, with others in New Mexico and the intermountain states, make it clear that the Fern Lake fire, for all its unique properties, was not exceptional.

This unsettling possibility was in the back of the Park Service's mind when in mid-June 2013 a lightning-ignited fire started in the Big Meadows sector of Rocky Mountain National Park. Even though the agency "preferred to allow naturally occurring fires to burn for the benefit of the resource and future fire breaks," the *Estes Park News* noted, it was concerned about "drought conditions and reduced interagency resources" that would limit its capacity to fight a "long duration fire." Remembering what happened in Forest Canyon, the Park Service moved quickly to suppress the flare-up.

Across the hotter and drier American West, this quick-strike tactic is becoming standard operating procedure, though it is a necessarily fraught compromise, for in slowing the fires' spread we will be retarding their key ecological function: to regenerate the region's distressed forests, to make green again these dark woods.

Message from the Eocene

Sometime 34 million years ago, a butterfly died, a nymphalid, today the largest family of butterflies (and perhaps then, too). Paleobiologists do not know how or why it perished. But that it lived is perfectly preserved in the geologic record.

More exactly, its fossilized remains were entombed in paper shale that has risen to the surface at what is now the Florissant Fossil Beds National Monument in Colorado. Once a shallow lake surrounded by groves of redwoods and broadleaf trees, a fecund home to a vibrant biota, the now-grassy site was buried in ash and lava flows from the once-volcanic mountains nearby. Over time, wind and erosion have swept away layers of this thick, pressurized coating: large silicified redwood trunks silently testify to the powerful natural forces that have transformed this terrain. The weathered, gray-black sheets of shale, and the paper-thin fossils embedded within them, bear witness to ancient life on earth.

This testimony is perhaps best captured in the excited prose of geologist Arthur C. Peale, who encountered the landscape in 1873: "When the mountains are

overthrown and the seas uplifted, the universe at Florissant flings itself against a gnat and preserves it."

Unearthing this deep past of butterflies and gnats,
fish, pollen, and tree trunks, all dazzling markers of the
Eocene Epoch, began in the nineteenth century as home-
steaders arrived in the area, some thirty miles outside
present-day Colorado Springs. In the 1870s, one of them—
Charlotte Hill—peeled back a layer of shale and spotted a
perfectly preserved fossil of a long-extinct butterfly, *Pro-
dryas persephone*. Like the specimen's mythic namesake,
Hill's discovery was immensely generative, rocking the
scientific world of her day.

A century later it still had the capacity to shake
things up: in the 1960s it was at the center of a sharp political debate pitting developers against an increasingly savvy
group of preservationists and paleontologists. Those who
wished to build upcountry chalets battled in the courts,
Congress, and the media against those who wanted
the federal government, through the good offices of the
National Park Service, to protect this spectacularly unique
remnant of a distant time. For the proponents of the fossil
beds, the long-dead butterfly still had wings.

We know the final outcome: on August 20, 1969,
after a bruising struggle that had more twists and turns
than any switchbacked trail up nearby Pike's Peak, President Richard Nixon signed legislation to "preserve and
interpret for the benefit and enjoyment of present and
future generations the excellently preserved insect and

leaf fossils and related geologic sites and objects" (Public Law 91-60). In doing so, he granted national monument status to a place some tout as the Rosetta Stone of North American paleontology.

Deciphering the tense maneuvering during the years and months that preceded the White House signing ceremony is an engrossing and wonderfully titled book, *Saved in Time*. Part memoir and part history, it is a collaborative project of Estella Leopold and Herbert Meyer. Leopold, a gifted paleobotanist and one of Aldo Leopold's remarkable progeny, joined forces with Meyer, a National Park Service paleontologist charged with interpreting the landscape that Leopold and the Defenders of Florissant fought hard to protect. Because their professional association with the site spans more than fifty years, their varied experiences eminently qualify them to identify this particular fossil bed's vital importance.

The question of its value, as so often happened in conservation battles of the 1950s and 1960s (and still), was framed between the scientific and cultural claims of the place set against those of growth and development. Like their contemporaries who fought against the construction of dams on free-flowing rivers or clear-cutting on national forests, and like their urban counterparts valiantly trying to block highways from blasting through historic neighborhoods and open space, the Defenders of Florissant faced nearly insurmountable odds.

The explosive economy of the postwar years, echoed in the demographic spike of the baby boom, privileged the arguments of those who promised to provide essential energy and other natural resources, to generate jobs and build homes. That ethos prevailed in small towns and major cities, in the civic arena, in politics and the law. To run against this American grain, to stop the bulldozers in their tracks, required an astonishing level of commitment and conviction.

Even then, conservationists did not always succeed. Growth for growth's sake, then as now, has a tenacious hold on the polity. So although scientists such as Estella Leopold and Beatrice Willard made an irrefutable case for the paleontological significance of Florissant, their arguments required the creation of a grassroots movement that would build an effective network of well-placed supporters in Colorado and across the nation. Their achievement depended as well on a team of skilled lawyers willing to work for a pittance to argue nonstop before judges at the local, state, and federal levels. They had the good fortune that their hue and cry was picked up by an emerging environmental movement and a sympathetic Congress then in the midst of promoting a series of initiatives, starting with the Wilderness Act of 1964; this legislation helped legitimize the idea that some pristine terrain was inviolable.

This broader cultural shift emboldened lawyers such as Richard Lamm, one of the attorneys active on the Florissant lawsuits, and later governor of Colorado: he and his peers "recognized that the laws were changing. It was really apparent by this time that there was going to be a whole new rethinking of the human role in the environment." In that ferment, Lamm reasoned, this particular case "was a risk worth taking."

However galvanizing the rhetoric proved to be, and as a rallying force it cannot be denied, the new federal legislation mostly was aimed at public-lands management. Had the Florissant fossil beds been on the public domain, the creation of the eponymous national monument would have been relatively easy. But they were located on private property, a status that intensified the legal pressure: urging the judiciary to prohibit owners from developing their land as they saw fit has never been an easy sell or a winning argument.

Surmounting this obstacle required a multifaceted attack. The Defenders of Florissant repeatedly went to court to delay developers eager to despoil the fossil beds for a housing subdivision, buying time so that its congressional allies could pass enabling legislation for national monument status complete with the monies necessary to purchase relevant acreage from willing sellers.

Yet when the courts dawdled and Congress fiddled, and the builders fired up the dozers to take matters in their own hands, activists had to get down and dirty, flinging their bodies in front of the diesel-spewing earth-moving equipment. As the drivers pulled back, the lawyers once more hustled into the courthouse.

The Defenders' legal team proved particularly adept at innovative pleadings. Most potent was its final gambit: they argued in federal court in July 1969 that the proposed "Florissant Monument is a national resource treasure" and that "the sovereign people of the United States" had a right to enjoy the fossil beds' "unique value," a right guaranteed under what attorney Victor Yannacone called the Public Trust Doctrine.

Dating back to colonial times, in which the British Crown decreed that it had an obligation to protect resources for public benefit, the doctrine found republican expression in the Ninth Amendment to the U.S. Constitution: "The enumeration in the Constitution, of certain rights, shall not be construed to deny or disparage others retained by the people."

At least that's how Yannacone parsed this arcane language, asserting boldly (and without precedent) that among the unenumerated rights this amendment protected is that of the people's to "the full benefit, use, and enjoyment of an irreplaceable natural resource."

Punctuating his assertion with a bit of John Muir–like hyperbole, Yannacone assured the courtroom that to "sacrifice this 34-million-year-old record, a record you might say written by the mighty hand of God, for 30-year mortgages and the basements of A-frame ghettos of the seventies is like wrapping fish with the Dead Sea Scrolls."

In the end, the federal court and Congress moved with just enough dispatch to preserve the land and its ancient artifacts. Ever since, the National Park Service has managed the monument on a tiny budget with few professional resources at its disposal, until Herbert Meyer became its first resident paleontologist in 1994. His painstaking work piecing together the local fossil record, in addition to cataloging and publishing a portion of the 35,000 specimens from Florissant now lodged in museums around the world, may be less dramatic than the cliffhanger campaign to defend the imperiled site, but it is no less critical. Without this voluminous evidence we'd have no real appreciation for just how important it was that one day, 34 million years ago, a butterfly died.

Cracked Arches

Moab, Utah, is a paradoxical place. The high desert community slotted into the canyonlands of the eastern portion of the Beehive State receives scant precipitation, yet through it surges one of the nation's great rivers, the mud-colored Colorado.

The millions of acre-feet of water that flow past the town each year have done little for those whose ambition has been to farm the dusty valley. The local economy also secured no discernible advantage from another of the area's natural features: back in the nineteenth century, when such things mattered enormously, Moab offered one of the few places that people and goods could safely ford the oft-rampaging river. Even that incentive was rendered inconsequential in 1883, the year the railroad penetrated the region, bypassing Moab well to the north: the village all but dried up.

Moab's saving graces are even more paradoxical, and strikingly visible, as you approach the city from the north on U.S. 191. On your left, the massive blocks of weathered, iron-rich red sandstone set off dramatically against the azure sky announce that you are nearing Arches National Park.

This staggering terrain draws more than 700,000 visitors annually, and they drop a lot of coin into the town's cash registers. But not one tourist can enter another federally managed site located about a mile or so south of the park's entrance, a place that once generated considerable work for and boomed the population of the region.

Squinting at the large sign planted in front of its gated drive, in type too small to read as we drove by, I barely deciphered the awkward acronym UMTRA. Google spelled it out for me: Uranium Mining Tailings Remedial Action project.

How disconcerting that the very same geological forces—an eons-long churn of uplift, erosion, sedimentation, and deposition—that generated the iconic monoliths, fins, and arches dazzling so many in the park also produced the mineral essential to the white-flash terror of atomic bombs. How odd that in Moab one federal agency sought to preserve wild nature and another, the Atomic Energy Commission (now the Nuclear Regulatory Commission), promoted the rapid exploitation of nature's rare-earth minerals to incinerate our enemies.

The tensions—cultural, environmental, and political—are every bit as complicated as they seem. In 1956 the Uranium Reduction Company built a uranium milling plant to the immediate northwest of Moab, on a site along whose southern border the Colorado runs. Its central product was the infamous yellowcake concentration, and until the mid-1980s it processed an estimated fourteen hundred tons a day. Sold exclusively to the Atomic Energy Commission until 1970, and subsequently to nuclear power plants, Moab's uranium punched up the nation's Cold War nuclear stockpiles and lit up millions of homes and businesses in the American West.

The tailings made Moab glow, and not in a good way. For nearly thirty years, the various companies that operated the facility dumped ton after ton of the radioactive sandy by-product into an unlined impoundment area located 750 feet from the river. Over the decades, this Geiger-hot waste, which ultimately totaled 12 million cubic yards, was spread over 130 acres at a depth of more than 80 feet. According to the Department of Energy (DOE), which took over remediation of the site, the tailings "have an average radioactivity of 665 picocuries per gram of radium-226," and because the center of the monstrous pile has a "high water content . . . excess water in the pile drains into under-lying soils, contaminating the ground water."

Some of the deleterious consequences are revealed in *The American West at Risk*, an illuminating book whose authors pay special attention to the Moab mill. It is hard to dispute their claim that this industrial site ranks "high in the annals of indiscriminate disposal," for the tailings each day continue to release "an estimated 28,000 gallons of radioactive pollutants and toxic chemicals into the only major river draining the southwestern United States."

Among the noxious by-products is ammonia, the levels of which are "several hundred times higher than state water quality standards allow and eight times the level considered lethal to fish." Add to this devastation the toxins absorbed by those who mined the radioactive material, inhaled wind-blown tailings dust, or just poured a cool drink of water on a blistering hot August afternoon.

The Moab mine, like Washington's Hanford Nuclear Reservation, Rocky Flats weapons facility in Colorado, and Los Alamos National Lab in New Mexico, helped turn the West into a radiant wasteland.

Cleaning up these hot spots requires a herculean effort, and because it is chronically short of funds, the DOE can only make slow progress in groundwater remediation. Slower still is the trans-shipment of tailings in steel canisters to a new storage facility in Crescent Junction, thirty miles north. Although the American Recovery and Reinvestment Act (2009) provided a critical infusion of money, those dollars were rapidly expended, and the department reports that currently it is only "shipping one train a day, 4 days a week, carrying up to 136 containers for a total of about 4,850 tons per trainload." It is going to take years before UMTRA completes its work, before Moab can breathe a huge sigh of relief.

Whether Moab should get a reprieve was for writer and critic Edward Abbey an open question. He liked to wallow in the apocalyptic, as his memoir of his experiences as a seasonal ranger in Arches National Park during the uranium rush of the 1950s suggests. "Let men in their madness blast every city on earth into black rubble and envelop the entire planet in a cloud of lethal gas," he wrote in *Desert Solitaire* (1968). The "canyons and hills, the springs and rocks will still be here, the sunlight will filter through, water will form and warmth shall be upon the land and after sufficient time . . . living things will emerge and join and stand once again, this time perhaps to take a different and better course."

For all his gleeful misanthropy—he never met a park visitor he did not abhor—Abbey wanted his readers to feel what he felt about this stark, jagged, and dry land, to sense its transcendence.

His words worked for me. Because two busloads of tourists had disembarked just before my wife and I pulled into the trailhead for Delicate Arch, we drove on to a remote overview, where Abbey's prose helped close the gap between where we stood and the formation we had come to see. This "weird, lovely, fantastic object out of nature . . . has the curious ability to remind us—like rock and sunlight and wind and wilderness—that *out there* is a different world, older and greater and deeper by far than ours, a world which surrounds and sustains the little world of men as sea and sky sustain a ship."

So buoyed, "we discover that nothing can be taken for granted, for if this ring of stone is marvelous all which shaped it is marvelous, and our journey here on earth, able to see and touch and hear in the midst of tangible and mysterious things-in-themselves, is the most strange and daring of all adventures."

But the journey is brief, as brief as that instant before the sun sets when the "voodoo monuments burn with a golden light, then fade to rose and blue and violet," and the "scarlet penstemon and the bayonets of the yucca turn dull and vague in the twilight."

Seeking Zion

On a late afternoon in Zion National Park, I stood on a pedestrian bridge spanning the Virgin River, a gentle arch over the snow-fed crystalline rush. The surge and clash of water on rock, a tumult of notes flat and sharp, somehow evoked Aldo Leopold's insights about the haunting timbre of cranes in flight.

"A dawn wind stirs the great marsh," he writes in *A Sand County Almanac*. This breath of air "rolls a bank of fog across the great morass" without a sound: "A single silence hangs from horizon to horizon." As the sky lightens, though, this preternatural quiet is shattered by "a pandemonium of trumpets, rattles, croaks, and cries that almost shakes the bog with its nearness, but without yet disclosing whence it comes. At last a glint of sun reveals the approach of a great echelon of birds. On motionless wing they emerge from the lifting mists, sweep a final arc of sky, and settle in clangorous descending spirals to their feeding grounds. A new day has begun on the crane marsh."

A day like countless others before it, Leopold affirmed. The cranes' honking echoes out of the "remote

Eocene," an impossible-to-imagine referent dating back 56 million years. "When we hear his call we hear no mere bird. We hear the trumpet in the orchestra of evolution. He is the symbol of our untamable past, of that incredible sweep of millennia which underlies and conditions the daily affairs of birds and men."

The icy waters sweeping beneath my feet, and their clangorous energy, make the same demand on our attention. After all, this river, and its many braided antecedents, has been at work since the Triassic, a mere 248 million years ago. That is when the site's oldest sandstone formation was laid down, to be overlaid periodically with new layers of rock, gravel, and sand that streams carried in from crumbling high ground, and more recently still by volcanic ash, gypsum, and shale, an incessant process of sedimentation and deposition truncated by periods of uplift and erosion.

Yet these earlier geological disruptions are not what have drawn so many visitors to Zion. Nor were they the reason President Taft signed legislation creating Mukuntuweap National Monument in 1909. (The National Park Service would delete its indigenous moniker nine years later, according to historian Hal K. Rothman, a consequence of the "prevalent bias of the time. Many believed that Spanish and Indian names would deter visitors who, if they could not pronounce the name of a place, might not bother to visit it. The new name, Zion, had greater appeal to an ethnocentric audience.")

No, what most struck the monument's proponents about this unique landform and to which Taft's proclamation obliquely refers—"the Mukuntuweap Canyon, through which flows the North Fork of the Rio Virgin, or Zion River, in Southwestern Utah, is an extraordinary example of canyon erosion and is of the greatest scientific interest"—was a product of the relatively more recent layer of Navajo sandstone.

The Virgin River has been carving through this iron oxide–rich material for eons, a force of nature that when combined with the erosive power of wind, and the sudden reconfigurations that earthquakes and rock slides can trigger, has left behind (and still sculpts) a baffling terrain.

"One hardly knows just how to think of it," observed artist Frederick S. Dallenbaugh in 1904. "Never before has such a naked mountain of rock entered into our minds! Without a shred of disguise its transcendent form rises preeminent. There is almost nothing to compare to it. Niagara has the beauty of energy; the Grand Canyon, of immensity; the Yellowstone, of singularity; the Yosemite, of altitude . . . this Great Temple, of eternity."

He has a point. Even about a section of the park as heavily visited as Emerald Pools. I got a sense of their eternal fascination while trailing behind a family of five; the tall, slender parents patiently herded three tow-headed daughters toward the lower pool.

When I first came upon them, the youngest was distraught. She had flung an acorn over the guardrail, an act she now regretted, as her sisters had held on to theirs. To cushion her jealous pang, her father suggested that maybe she had helped plant a tree. His was a deft resolution that drew a comforted smile.

How perfect that a toddler might create new life in a valley containing some of the region's oldest soils.

By the time the boisterous brood had reached the small pool, fed with spray from the upslope ledge, the parents had slipped hats on their progeny's small heads to protect them from the light mist. No sooner had they reached the heaviest fall, though—a cool shower on this hot June day—than Mom and Dad urged their children to look up. The kids shrieked; their faces glistened.

"A facial," their mother laughed. A geological scrub, I thought, a ritual cleanse, a baptismal kiss.

More immersed in this place are the canyon tree frogs, whose resounding racket bounced off the rippled sandstone walls, magnifying these amphibians' claim to niche and mate. Their insistent bleating followed me up the stone-stepped path worn down by thousands of feet, and intensified when I reached the middle pond, only to double in volume as I clambered over boulders and dropped into the bowl that cupped the upper pond's still waters.

Passersby chortled: "They're so horny."

Can you blame them? Their reproductive urge, circumscribed by their narrowed opportunities to attract and couple, vibrated in the thin air. Like the primeval blare of Leopold's cranes, these frogs' booming pleas are "wild-ness incarnate."

The shadowed rock face that towers above asserts an even more ancient claim. It has been forever stained by falling water, a chiseling flow that hones the dark edge of deep time.

Sea Change: An Afterword

The road west was filled with signs and wonders. Like the hill-hugging black squall that slammed into us as we drove up into the wrinkled folds of the Edwards Plateau in central Texas. Like the ominous dark funnel cloud that swirled along the highway in the arid, far-western reaches of the Lone Star State, scattering cattle and cars. Close to the Arizona-California border, a flatbed truck erupted into a fireball as we sped past.

What in the world were we heading into?

The most compelling answer lay not in nature's climatic power or human accident. Rather, the real portent seemed lodged in the Union Pacific's shiny tracks running parallel to Interstate 10. As we followed the sun down that concrete roadbed, moving in the opposite direction was a steady stream of freight trains loaded with double-stacked containers. These color-coded, forty-foot steel units bore their owners' logos: Maersk, Hanjin, China Shipping. Globalization was on the move.

I've thought about this wide-angled panorama—mile-long trains rumbling up slope and down, thundering around wide curves—every time I drive past the intimidatingly large Colton rail yard in Southern California. It is the central hub of the regional goods movement, located in the heart of the Inland Empire, a sprawled stretch of valley that spreads across San Bernardino and Riverside Counties sixty miles east of Los Angeles. Each day hundreds of eighteen-wheelers swing off the 10 and 60 freeways to offload containers they have hauled from the ports of Long Beach and Los Angeles for trans-shipment east by rail.

The tremendous amount of commerce flowing through this node, for all its economic benefits, comes with decided local costs: the polluted air, deafening noise, and jack-hammer-like vibrations it generates compromise the health and well-being of the adults and children who live on its periphery. The city of Ontario, cut in half by the railroad and CA-60, suffers from the highest levels of air pollution and associated diseases such as asthma of any community in the Southland.

By its very nature, globalization creates sacrifice zones like Ontario and Colton, places and populations that disproportionately bear the brunt of our consuming desires and that are further buffeted by a political economy that can so cavalierly rearrange lives and landscapes.

Such injustice has long been true for all species inhabiting this region, a reality that is woven through *Not So Golden State.* But it took that most academic of settings—a conference panel at the 2012 meeting of the American Society for Environmental History—to make its impact achingly obvious. I served as chair and commentator for a session titled "Transnational Labor and the Environment" and thus listened as my colleagues addressed some of the early manifestations of globalization in the Pacific World, a process that also disrupted that almost-indelible east-to-west orientation of the narrative Americans routinely employ to describe how our nation expanded: westward, the course of empire.

Begin in California, then, with the Russian construction of Fort Ross, founded in 1808 as an agricultural depot for the czar's imperial outposts in Alaska; this western Pacific empire, as Melinda Herrold-Menzies noted, was establishing a critical toehold on the ocean's eastern coast. To be successful, however, Russia required cheap and plentiful labor, and its military rounded up Alaska Natives to serve its economic interests in what would become Sonoma County. Despite this coerced crew's best efforts, the initiative failed miserably, as the site's soils, temperatures, and moisture levels frustrated grain production.

Enter the sea otter: Russian merchants shifted the focus of Fort Ross's mission to that animal's slaughter and subsequent curing of its lustrous pelt for sale in China. Otter fur brought such high prices there that nearby coastal populations were swiftly decimated. Hunters began to move south in search of new sources, and so efficient was the killing on- and offshore that within thirty years or so the California sea otter was on the brink of extinction; the kelp forests this keystone carnivore maintained were also in a state of collapse. Brutal labor practices had been twinned with an equally rough ecological manipulation to power the emerging cross-Pacific trade networks of the early nineteenth century.

These fraught interconnections and implications became even more punitive in the coming decades as British, American, Russian, Canadian, and Japanese fleets chased down whales, seals, and salmon throughout the northern Pacific. The pursuit of oil, fur, and meat promoted the industrialization of fishing, accelerated the destruction of these once-plentiful species, pushed remote native villages into the globalizing culture of production and consumption, and troubled international relations.

These "tentacles of contact," as historian Lissa Wadewitz calls them, linked together far-flung ports and the open sea, demonstrated how profit, disease, and destitution could follow in the wake of the many vessels that crisscrossed the bounding main, and revealed as well a perplexing geopolitics that led to some startling adaptations.

Confronted with nation-states that used their naval power to protect what they considered to be their marine resources, owners of fishing vessels often would register their ships in the relevant countries to flummox authorities. Because sailors who shipped out under a particular flag were considered its subjects under international marine law, this allowed them to continue to work even if their homeland was banned from Japanese or Russian or American waters. Only when it dawned on these contentious nations that they were extirpating the invaluable species they so diligently hunted did they meet over the negotiating table in 1911 to settle some of their differences.

There have been no such international negotiations framed around the status and rights of late twentieth-century migrant labor so essential to the regeneration of clear-cut forests in the Pacific Northwest. Making that case is Brinda Sarathy, whose *Pineros: Latino Labour and the Changing Face of Forestry in the Pacific Northwest* has compelled us to rethink the linkages between economic development, environmental management, and social justice.

"In the shadowy realms of the forest today, one will rarely find the white logger or the environmental activist," she declared. "Rather, one may run into the likes of Juan Cabrera, an undocumented immigrant from Zacatecas, Mexico, who crossed the border at sixteen and has been tree planting on federal lands ever since. One may chance upon Pedro Zamora Gómez, who was struck by an errant tree limb while thinning overgrown stands of fir, suffered a debilitating back injury, and was left to cope without health care."

These individuals and their many peers constitute the bulk of contracted manual labor operating on the region's public and private forests. Like their predecessors during the Great Depression, and later via the Bracero Program of the 1940s and 1950s, they have taken on backbreaking jobs for low wages and minimal benefits, a south-to-north movement of labor that has been central to the local production of wood fiber for international consumption.

Recovering their lived experiences, to make the invisible visible, Sarathy conducted interviews with forest workers, thereby giving human shape to their struggles and making active those whom "history" too often presumes to have been but acted upon. By listening in on their laments and laughter, we can also better imagine the relationship between their difficult situations and that of others who long ago were pressed into service in the Russian colonial experiment or who wielded harpoon, net, or club to serve the needs of the burgeoning transpacific marketplace.

Yet these stories, for all their explanatory power, do not constitute the full chronological arc of this vast ocean's internationalization, or the way they set the stage for many of the environmental challenges that have since confronted this wider region. Their launch, indeed, can be backdated at least to 1565, when the first wind-driven Spanish galleons began plying the waters between Manila and Acapulco. What those initial voyages set in motion was a pattern of economic activity and resource exploitation that continues to play out every time a diesel-powered Union Pacific engine pulls away from the Colton rail yard, thundering east.

Acknowledgments

Every book is a collaborative process, and this book is no exception to that rule. At its core is a series of journeys across California and the West, and I could not imagine a more fun and compelling companion on road, trail, or water than Judi Lipsett. For more than forty years we have poked around this region—and a lot of other places—and in the process built a marriage and family; these acknowledgments must begin with her because everything does.

Zach Behrens, who read many of these chapters as editor of KCET.org, and who now happily applies his craft for the National Park Service, pushed me to make my prose more accessible to a wider audience, a key aim of this book. I am grateful to Dean Betsy Crighton, the Office of Academic Affairs, and the Pomona College Faculty Research Fund, for timely support of this project. Over the years, Mark Kendall and Cindy Peters have done so much to help me get my writing before a larger readership. In the Claremont Colleges Consortium, much of our intellectual life revolves around the Honnold/Mudd Libraries, and I am indebted to their remarkable crew of librarians, past and present, including Char Booth, Lisa Crane, Jessica Greene,

Carrie Marsh, Adam Rosenkranz, and Sean Stone, as well as the Dean of the Library, Kevin Mulroy. Like my stellar colleagues in the five-college major in environmental analysis, they have shared books and articles, documents and illustrations. For them all, ideas matter—a lot—and I (and my students) are the lucky beneficiaries of their collective engagement.

The same can and should be said of the amazing editors/writers at Trinity University Press. This is my fifth project that founding director, poet Barbara Ras, has shepherded to publication, and every one of them is the better for her keen eye and wise advice and, best of all, her friendship. Barbara's colleagues have become friends, too: thanking Tom Payton, Sarah Nawrocki, Burgin Streetman, Lee Ann Sparks, and Steffanie Mortis is not enough, but it is a start. The comments of the two anonymous readers were spot on, and I have incorporated many of their smart suggestions.

Not So Golden State got its start with another San Antonio connection: several years after Gary Kates left Trinity, where we had taught together for twenty years, to become dean at Pomona College, he invited me to spend a year teaching in its environmental analysis (EA) program. That's when I met geologist Rick Hazlett, EA's coordinator and driving force; his intellectual range is as broad as his energy is intimidating (don't expect to beat him up rugged Mount Baldy, which at 10,000 feet towers over Claremont; it cannot be done, as many an athletic undergrad will attest). He has been a formative presence in my work here as a teacher and scholar, and remains so in his retirement. I am delighted to express my gratitude for his kind, patient, and generous mentoring by dedicating this book to him.

Char Miller, formerly a professor of history at Trinity University, is director of the environmental analysis program and W. M. Keck Professor of Environmental Analysis at Pomona College. He is the author of the award-winning *Gifford Pinchot and the Making of Modern Environmentalism*; *On the Edge: Water, Immigration, and Politics in the Southwest*; *Deep in the Heart of San Antonio: Land and Life in South Texas*; *Public Lands, Public Debates: A Century of Controversy*; and *America's Great National Forests, Wildernesses, and Grasslands*. He is the editor of *On the Border: An Environmental History of San Antonio* and *Fifty Years of the* Texas Observer. He lives in Claremont.